SAPPER MARTIN

Thirty-one-year-old Admiralty clerk Albert John (Jack) Martin was called up into the army in 1916. It was forbidden to keep diaries during his service with the Royal Engineers (the Sappers). However, the secret diaries he wrote then, remained undiscovered until 1999. Jack Martin's compelling record presents the reality of war: from his arrival in France during the Battle of the Somme, through the onslaught at Ypres and the German offensive of 1918, to the Armistice, we see how the ordinary Tommy lived and fought. Martin describes the appalling conditions in which the men lived and died — and the support of friends and joy at the arrival of parcels from loved ones. An exceptional discovery, these diaries have been edited by First World War historian Richard van Emden.

Books by Richard van Emden
Published by The House of Ulverscroft:

THE SOLDIER'S WAR

Edited by
RICHARD VAN EMDEN

◆

SAPPER MARTIN

The Secret Great War Diary of Jack Martin

Complete and Unabridged

CHARNWOOD
Leicester

First published in Great Britain in 2009 by
Bloomsbury Publishing Plc, London

First Charnwood Edition
published 2010
by arrangement with
Bloomsbury Publishing Plc, London

British Library CIP Data

Martin, Jack.
    Sapper Martin: the secret Great War diary of
Jack Martin.
    1. Martin, Jack- -Diaries.
    2. World War, *1914 – 1918-* -Personal narratives, British.
    3. World War, *1914 – 1918-* -Campaigns- -Western
Front. 4. Large type books.
    I. Title II. Van Emden, Richard.
    940.4'81'41–dc22

    ISBN 978–1–44480–356–3

Published by
F. A. Thorpe (Publishing)
Anstey, Leicestershire

Set by Words & Graphics Ltd.
Anstey, Leicestershire
Printed and bound in Great Britain by
T. J. International Ltd., Padstow, Cornwall

This book is printed on acid-free paper

Dedicated to Peter and Maggie Barton
and Jeremy and Clair Banning

I am now on night duty. Sitting by the firelight has grown oppressive so I have lit a precious candle to enable me to pass the time in writing. I have been outside the billet and the silence is the sort that can be felt. People who live under modern conditions of civilisation can scarcely comprehend the meaning of absolute silence. And the silence of the trenches among the mountains is almost palpable.

Outside the billet I looked towards the line and listened for any sounds of war of contending armies but the absolute quiet was not broken even by a 'beetles droning flight'. There is not the least sign of life or activity and the winking stars look down like the cynical eyes of cruel gods ready to laugh at human suffering and misery. Yet you know well enough that away in front men are ceaselessly watching ready to give the alarm at the first sign of animation on the enemy's lines; and there are rifles and machines guns and trench mortars and field guns and howitzers of all kinds and sizes ready to break forth into a clamorous roaring and screeching at any moment. And there may be added the drone of aeroplanes and the rushing of wagons and motor lorries and the rattle and banging of railway trains and many other incidental noises.

You know that all this noise is possible and the

Silence makes you shudder. It feels uncanny. It oppresses you. You whistle for sake of company but your own whistle makes you start and the Silence following the momentary break seems stranger and more awesome than before. So you creep back into your billet with cold shivering down your spine and a dull nervousness in your heart. And there you have a light and you see your comrades asleep, and hear their snorings and inarticulate grunting and you feel like being at home once more. Your spine becomes warm and erect — your heart steady and brave, and you say 'Bah! I wasn't afraid; I was only interested.'

Jack Martin, 9/1/18

Contents

Introduction

Is it simply too easy to suggest that a man who fought on and survived the Western Front was 'lucky'? The word appears to offer a quick, casual distinction between those who were killed or seriously wounded and those who came home apparently whole. How can 'lucky' begin truly to explain an individual's remarkable escape from shell splinters that fell next to, or ripped past, his body? How can 'luck' justly explain the bullets that cracked past his head, time and time again, never finding their mark, belying all the apparent odds? Yet it is the right word, because there is no rational explanation. In the end only 'luck' amply explains the sheer randomness and utter injustice of war that could leave a man standing after four years of fighting, and take another who had only just arrived in the trenches.

In January 1917, Sapper Albert (Jack) Martin, four months into his service on the Western Front, wondered at his luck when a shell just skimmed the top of the dugout in which he had been sitting and exploded in a neighbouring one, killing a fellow Royal Engineer. 'A piece of the shell [had] passed clean through his body close to his heart,' Martin noted in his private diary. 'He had only come out just before Xmas and his comrades had envied him as having a safe 'cushy' job.'

Jack Martin was to remain a lucky man. He managed to survive more than two uninterrupted years on the Western and Italian fronts, and received nothing more than a 'cat's claw' scratch in all the time he was in or near the front line during some of the most intense battles of the Great War. Perhaps he was luckiest of all in that he was constitutionally a man who could compartmentalise his war, able to move on from all that he had experienced, all the degradation and suffering he had witnessed, to live a contented and fulfilled life. For this reason alone, he was one of the Great War's true survivors, damaged neither physically nor mentally; he was not obsessive about his service, unlike so many others, did not flail about in his sleep, or jump or duck at the backfiring of a car. He did not suddenly weep, or moodily sulk. His temper remained even; he was happy.

This is not to say that Jack Martin forgot his past. He remembered his comrades on Armistice Day but then moved on. According to his surviving son, Peter, an eighty-eight-year-old veteran of the Second World War, he tried to put the Great War at the back of his mind, not always successfully, but he certainly escaped its malign influence that haunted so many others for the rest of their days.

His lasting contribution to the memory of the war is in the form of twelve diaries of exceptional quality and depth. Like all diaries illicitly kept by both officers and soldiers during the war (for they were, like cameras, banned), it was not meant for public consumption but was left as a meticulous record of one man's service. Was it written for his family, or was it a way of putting his war to bed, once and for all? Nobody knows, for he never spoke about it. From the date that he transcribed his diaries (probably in 1922) until his death, the diaries remained hidden and were never mentioned to family or friends. In fact, even after Jack Martin's death nearly forty years ago, the diaries did not immediately come to light. Bundled up with a heap of odds and ends, they were kept in a large black plastic bin bag, undiscovered until a decade ago when Peter found and read them.

The original wartime diaries were apparently not preserved, and in fact very little was known of Jack Martin's war. No discharge papers survived and only two photographs, one taken shortly before Jack left for France, the other in post-war Germany where Jack served briefly with the Army of Occupation. Even his two service medals have disappeared.

Jack was born Albert John Martin at Fakenham, near the north Norfolk coast, on 3 September 1884, one of three brothers and four sisters. He was a sickly infant. He was once given up for dead when he was just a few months old, and his parents drew the blinds as an indication to the outside world that somebody had died. No one now knows what his illness was.

His father was a Methodist minister who, in that capacity, moved his family around Britain every three years to a new circuit. The upheaval was considerable, the family moving

3

from as far away as a mining village in South Wales to Gravesend in Kent. Jack's father, according to his grandson Peter, 'was probably pacifist and very liberal, at least he liked to think he was liberal, liberal in a way, but fierce at home where he was a strict disciplinarian. A self-righteous man, his evils were debt, dirt, drink and the Devil . . . and the *Daily Mail*.'

Comics were utterly prohibited when Jack was a boy; his father, a humourless man, would not have them in the house. Playtime at school was being marched around by the local recruiting sergeant, though at home toy soldiers were forbidden by his father. Jack's humour came from his mother, who was an altogether different personality; she wrote poems and she had emotions that were quite different from those of her husband.

As a young boy, Jack learnt to play the piano and then played the harmonium for his father's Sunday services; he had to listen to the same sermon three times a day at different churches. Peter commented that his father later called himself a nonconformist but wasn't aligned to any church in particular.

Jack's father died in August 1916; his relationship with his son had never been close. Nevertheless, Jack was like the older man in one way: he was a believer in self-help and, although he left school at fourteen, he educated himself. He had some lessons on the piano, but was largely self-taught; he also taught himself law and accountancy even though he had no further formal teaching at all. Financial circumstances

4

meant there was never any possibility of his going to university.

When he left school, Jack was persuaded to take the Civil Service Boys' Exam and went into the Admiralty, presumably as a clerk. As a young man in London, he lived with Mr and Mrs Berwick, who owned a boarding house. He became good friends with them and frequently noted their generosity in his diaries, receiving a number of letters and food parcels while serving overseas.

Apart from his immediate family and the Berwicks, Jack refers in his diaries most often to Elsie. Jack met Elsie Kate Brewster in London around 1910 and they were engaged, but did not marry until June 1919. Their son Peter suspects that they thought it wasn't right to get married just because war was coming, and they would see it through, as they did. Perhaps, too, Jack did not wish to leave Elsie a war widow, a plight suffered by so many others.

Jack joined the army in early 1916, and felt it right that he should go. Aged thirty-one, he was a patriotic man, firmly patriotic, clearly feeling that the British nation was a cut above everyone else. He was the only member of the family to serve; one brother died before the war and the other was in a reserved occupation. It is probably fair to say that he did not like the army, he did not like most officers, he did not like being told what to do by people he felt were his mental inferiors. His son does not think that he ever sought promotion or was ever particularly offered it, although he ended the war as a lance corporal.

Jack Martin made a reluctant but idiosyncratic soldier. He played the organ, quoted from *Tristram Shandy* and carried a copy of Shakespeare's *The Merchant of Venice* for preferred reading. He was chosen to stage-manage army events when out of the front line, and, when time and a cloudless sky permitted, he waxed lyrical to anyone who would listen, about astronomy and the constellations they could see: he was, it is fair to say, no ordinary Tommy.

Yet, at the same time, that is exactly what he was. Sapper Martin, a sometimes grumbling, grousing 'other rank'; a man who stood by his mates through the worst that war could throw at him. At times he kept going although shell-shocked, with shaking hand, gaunt face and a profound depth of fatigue that haunted his waking hours. When finally relieved he slept, indifferent to the chaos of his surroundings, unruffled by the discomfort of his 'bed'.

Sapper Martin belied his lowly rank. Erudite and articulate, he kept his diary throughout his service in France from the moment he left Great Britain to the moment of demobilisation two and a half years later. Despite the ban on soldiers keeping diaries, a restriction that was widely broken, he carefully noted the day's events in notebooks that grew in number from one to twelve, rarely missing a day.

Probably owing to his obvious intelligence, he was chosen to be a signaller in the Royal

Engineers, and a very proficient one he turned out to be. His job did not consist merely of taking encoded messages sent from various parts of the line; he was frequently expected to leave the dugout and pass across the battlefield, maintaining communications when telephone lines had been cut in many places by shell fragments.

The diary reflected each day. Nevertheless, it would be surprising if, during the intense horror of an attack, he wrote much about his experiences; indeed, it would have been a dereliction of duty had he done so. After all, the lives of hundreds if not thousands of men were held in the balance, and success or failure in an attack could depend on the one intact telephone line that led back from a muddy hole in a battle-scarred wasteland all the way to Corps Headquarters. For that reason, he regularly updated his diary, sometimes days later, going back over recent events. In the main, however, he sought out quiet moments when he could jot down his thoughts, sometimes, when times were quiet, at a length of several pages.

There are some frustrating aspects to the story. Did Jack actually know that soldiers were forbidden to keep diaries during the war? If so, did he go to great pains to hide the fact that he was keeping one? It would not have been easy, given the amount that he managed to write, and it is possible his Commanding Officer chose to turn a blind eye. Certainly, he took risks: he divulged information that might have been useful to the enemy, giving, for example, the names of towns and villages, and repeating conversations he heard between senior officers. It is possible, of course, that he originally used a code, especially as he records using one in his letters to Elsie, letting her know in this way where he was at the time. As the original diaries have not survived, we shall never know.

Sadly, Jack Martin's enlistment papers no longer exist, either. Around 70 per cent of all records were destroyed in an enemy raid in the Second World War (the remainder are held at the National Archives) so details of precisely when he enlisted are not known, nor even where he trained. It is very likely that he enlisted either under the Derby Scheme (a scheme by which men could volunteer and then return to civilian employment until required) or that he was called up shortly after conscription was introduced in January 1916. He had no previous knowledge of or training in signals (he was never a member of the Scouts, for example) and so he must surely have received a minimum of six months' instruction before being ordered overseas.

During his army career, Jack was particularly close to Private Stuart Thomas Glasspoole, known as Tom, who, like Jack, had been a clerk, working for the Pearl Assurance Company in London. Jack refers to Glasspoole throughout his diary, with obvious affection. He was ten years younger than Jack, and was only twenty-two when he arrived in France. He had enlisted in the Surrey Yeomanry in 1913 and transferred to the 12th Battalion East Surrey Regiment after the outbreak of war. We do not know whether Jack knew Tom before their service overseas. However, they embarked within five days of each other in September 1916 and were demobbed within ten days of each other in February 1919.

Perhaps the most interesting relationship that Jack Martin had was with his Commanding Officer, Lieutenant, later Captain, Buchanan. Fletcher Gordon Buchanan came from Glasgow and went to France in May 1916, aged twenty-seven. He served with the 122nd Infantry Brigade Signals, to which Martin was sent, until he was transferred to 39th Division Headquarters as a signalling officer in July 1917. His sojourn there was short, as he was injured only three weeks later when he was knocked off his motorcycle by a shell explosion. He received shrapnel wounds to head, arm and leg, though none was considered serious. We do not know whether he returned to France. However, he was forced to resign his commission in January 1919 owing to ill health. Lieutenant Buchanan had, as Jack Martin's diary shows, made an offer to the men under his command that if they needed help after the war they were to call on him at his business address and he would endeavour to do what he could for them. It is not clear exactly what Buchanan did, but it appears that he had business interests in eastern India.

Jack's relationship with Buchanan was fraught. His attitude to officers, especially those who did not come up to the mark, was ambiguous to say the least. However, Jack respected Buchanan but could not understand why his Commanding

Officer was difficult with him, always pointing out supposed errors or failures. Normally, Jack would have cared little for what an officer thought but with Buchanan it was different. The desire to win this officer's commendation was strong and when Buchanan finally accepted him, the depth of feeling elicited from Jack was unprecedented.

Unlike some veterans who walked away from all connections to their service, Jack was friendly for many years with his comrades in arms. Jack's son Peter met up with several: Glasspoole was one, and there was another from Halifax. With one old friend he actually crossed the Channel and went back to Belgium; it was against his own wishes and all his inclinations, as Peter recalls. 'Jack didn't want to go, but he went just to please this man. They were there only a day and possibly a night and they came back, and he had not enjoyed it. 'What's the point?' he said. It didn't do anything for him.' He never went again.

He thought about the war, Peter remembers, but he didn't want to think about it. It was an aspect of his life that he had not exactly turned his back on but wanted to ignore, to forget about. He was quite keen on respecting Armistice Day, though he didn't go to church then. Nor did he ever wear his medals, definitely not. We don't know what happened to them but I suspect he just threw them away; I've never come across them. As for the diaries: I suppose he wanted me and my children to know about what it was like.

'I asked him one or two things but he never opened up. The diaries were how he communicated his feelings. I knew hardly anything, except that he was on the Somme and that he had gone to Italy. I knew he'd seen tanks, and that gas had been blown into the trenches where he was, but they had a damp blanket across the doorway to keep it out. I don't think he minded me asking, but he was not naturally forthcoming about it. Reading the diaries I found he didn't come across as any different from the man I knew. He may have mellowed in the 1920s, he may have been less uptight. He could just close the door on that part of his life and start again with my mother's help.'

What would he feel about his diaries being published? 'I don't think he would care one way or the other; he wouldn't be embarrassed, in fact on the whole I think he would be pleased but I don't think he would be overjoyed. He didn't express much emotion. He never said 'I love you' to me, like I do to my children, and I didn't hear him say that to my mother although he must have loved her. That was his innate nature, the war had not taken emotion from him. He was very much his own man.'

After Jack Martin returned to civilian life he took a job in Beckenham, Kent, with a company that made electrical motors. It was not a long-term job. In the spirit of self-education to which Martin had always subscribed, he studied and qualified as a certified accountant, before becoming self-employed in the late 1920s. He set up a practice, eventually taking his only child,

Peter, into partnership. He continued to work until shortly after his wife Elsie died in January 1964, retiring the following year aged eighty. Jack then lived with his son's family in Basingstoke. He died on 24 April 1970 aged eighty-five.

Jack Martin has made my job as editor not only a highly enjoyable one, for he is such a good writer, but also a relatively easy one. His stories are frequently self-explanatory and at times I have had little more to do than to clarify abbreviations. While editing the book, (about a third of the original text has been deleted), it was evident which passages might be cut to avoid repetition and only during the third and final fine cut did the process prove at all tricky.

As editor I had to make the decision when to interject into proceedings and whether my words would seem more like an interruption than a help. In the end I felt that my role was to let Jack tell his story in as pure a way as possible and so I have restricted myself to a full introduction and then, as far as the text is concerned, simply setting Jack's words into their historical context.

There are, of course, many well-written diaries about the Great War, from the classics by Graves and Sassoon to lesser known ones that were nevertheless beautifully written. They are, in the main, written by officers. Far fewer are by other ranks, and, of those that exist, none, to my knowledge, are written by Royal Engineers, except for this one. But here is a brilliantly written book, penned, unusually, by another rank who happened to be a signaller. However, what gives this book an extra dimension is the beguiling character of the man himself, a cautious and meticulous character who wrote diaries of remarkable insight and sensitivity but also, perhaps most surprisingly, of easy and natural humour. Jack Martin was a man brimming with curiosity, full of life and vigour; a man who was utterly honest in what he wrote. The old adage 'still waters run deep' was never better exemplified than in him.

Jack Martin served with the 122nd Infantry Brigade Signal Company, part of the 41st Division. He wore the camp badge of the Royal Engineers, perhaps one of the most overlooked regiments of the British Army when it comes to written history. This is ironic for they were never overlooked during the Great War. On the contrary, their presence on the battlefield was absolutely vital not just for the successful prosecution of war but for war to be waged at all. As the conflict grew increasingly industrial in nature, so the regiments that reflected that change grew as a proportion of the army as a whole. For example, Heavy Artillery grew from 1.3 per cent of the army's strength to over 8.5 per cent by 1918; the Royal Engineers grew from roughly 6 to 12 per cent. Conversely, the cavalry shrank from 10 to just 2 per cent and even the infantry, their numbers swelled by voluntary enlistment and conscription, shrank as a proportion of the army from 65 to 50 per cent.

The REs grew from a little over 25,000 officers and men in August 1914, including regular, reserve and territorial troops, to over 295,000 just three years later. Of these, 19,794 were to die in the war and sixteen Victoria Crosses were won.

It was, and remains, a simple fact that the British Army could not function without the Royal Engineers. They acted as the glue that kept the army's constituent parts together, and the oil to ensure that all parts worked well. Their motto *Ubique* (Everywhere) amply described their presence on the battlefield, both in the front line, building and reconstructing (as well as demolishing) positions and fortifications, transporting and constructing pontoons and bridges, very often under intense fire, and behind the front line, building and maintaining roads, railways and waterways.

As well as being ultimately responsible for the large-scale infrastructure of the battlefield, they maintained key elements vital to the army's overall success. They were responsible for all communications, maintaining telephone lines, wireless and all other equipment used for signalling. They ensured a water supply to the trenches through miles of pipes, hundreds of water tanks and butts filled from temporary reservoirs supplied from bore holes. In the line, they were in charge of tunnelling operations, digging shafts and burrowing deep beneath the ground to lay explosives under enemy trenches. Field Survey companies located enemy positions, through sound ranging and flash spotting, so that accurate fire could be laid down, and, after the enemy's first use of poison gas, special gas companies were formed to engage the enemy in the deadly art of gas warfare.

14

The Royal Engineers quarried, drained and bored; they surveyed the topography of the ground, and studied meteorology, forecasting the weather for the senior command. They were responsible for forestry, chopping down trees for myriad purposes, including the duckboard tracks that wended their way across the battlefield, the assault ladders that would take the men over the top, and the wood used to line and prop a trench.

Everything that was used to construct the defences upon which the infantry relied was tried and tested by the Royal Engineers, right down to the strength and durability of the nails that held everything together: the list goes on and on. It is hardly surprising, then, that the Royal Engineers grew in number throughout the war as their overall remit was massively expanded.

Sapper Martin was the smallest cog in an enormous and expanding wheel. But his job, as a signaller with Brigade Headquarters, was more important than that of any corresponding infantryman, trooper or gunner, for the lives of hundreds, perhaps thousands, of men could rely on his accurate message taking, on his courage to mend a telephone line cut by shrapnel, or his willingness to stay awake and mentally alert when his body craved sleep. It was a heavy responsibility, and he knew it and responded to the challenge.

THE DIARY

1916

Sunday 17.9.16
Left Hitchin just before 9 a.m. Saw Elsie at her window as we marched to the station. Embarked at Southampton at 4 p.m.

18.9.16
Disembarked at Rouen about 6 a.m. Marched past numbers of German prisoners working in the streets, to a barbed-wire compound where we got some breakfast at a YMCA hut. Crowded with men either going up to or coming down from the line. Played a number of ragtime choruses on the piano. Later I was fetched to play hymns for a service. The chaplain gave me a Testament that I retained until sent home for demobilisation. Medical exam and then entrained.

19.9.16
Arrived at Abbeville after a most uncomfortable journey (thirty-six in a truck) early in the morning. Marched to the Signal Depot where we caught up some of the men who had left Hitchin a few days before we did.

20.9.16–22.9.16
Did not have much to do at Abbeville and each
evening we were allowed out. Could not go in
the Cathedral but saw the massive doors which
are its pride. Don't think much of the city
— some parts are very low, and probably the
present circumstances of being a military centre
have dragged it lower.

23.9.16
This morning my name appeared on orders to
proceed to the 41st Division. I leave tonight and
anticipate finding myself on the Somme
tomorrow.

The Battle of the Somme was a campaign essen-
tially conceived out of political necessity. The
idea was to show that the British and French
could not only launch a successful campaign
together but that they could fight alongside one
another in a show of military solidarity. That was
the primary reason why, in late 1915, the gently
rolling chalk downland of the Somme region was
chosen as the 'best' place to force a decision on
the Western Front in 1916. Hitherto, the area
had been little more than a Franco-German back-
water where little actual fighting had taken place.
The British had arrived in the summer of
1915, not necessarily to fight in the region but
rather to take over more of the front line that
stretched all the way from the Belgian coast to
the Swiss Alps. The French had been holding by
far the greater proportion and as the number of

British troops serving overseas grew exponentially in the spring and summer of 1915, so it was felt appropriate that Britain should shoulder a greater responsibility not just in terms of fighting but simply holding the line. Only after the British had arrived on the Somme did the idea of a joint offensive begin to germinate. In February 1916 the Germans attacked the French at Verdun and, as more and more French servicemen were drawn into the fighting further south, so their commitment to a Somme offensive was much curtailed. Indeed, such was the ferocity of the fighting at Verdun that the British were increasingly urged, then implored, to fight at the earliest possible moment so as to draw off German forces from the beleaguered town. The British would put an enormous effort into what optimistically became known as the 'Big Push'. A huge preliminary bombardment followed by a heavy infantry assault would, over days and then weeks, throw back the Germans across French-held territory. The outcome, as it was sold to the British public, was that this was an offensive that might end the war.

Reality was rarely the equal of expectation in the Great War and a catastrophic failure on the first day of the battle was only partially redeemed by limited success in the weeks and months that followed. Success would soon be measured in hundreds of yards rather than in dozens of miles, as each wood, each village and each roadway was contested by British troops determined to take the land in equal proportion to the Germans' desire not to relinquish it.

In September 1916 the British introduced a new secret weapon, the tank. This seemed to hold out the prospect of renewed success, but although the Germans were taken by surprise at its appearance, once again the battle stalled. It was just days after the advent of the tank that Jack Martin arrived in France, to be quickly sent forward to join his unit in the line. As a signaller with the 41st Division, a unit used in some of the tanks' first assaults, he would quickly get to see all the horror of modern warfare and the skeletal debris of both man and knocked-out tank close to the front line.

24.9.16
Travelling. We left Abbeville in the usual crowded cattle trucks at 9.30 last night. In the morning we were near Amiens. Progress is frightfully slow. Sometimes there were as many as five trains all crawling close behind each other. There may have been more round the bends. Every time we stopped near any orchards some of the fellows would jump out and fetch apples. Two or three got left behind just as we entered the tunnel before Amiens but they walked over the top and caught us up at the other end. Stace, another fellow named Morgan, and I were booked for the 41st Division. We were told to get out at Edge Hill which is the railhead. We found a Middlesex guide who said he would take us to our Division. He walked us right up to Fricourt where we saw the big guns in action for the first time, but after tramping about for some

time without finding any trace of the Div. we decided to pad it back to Edge Hill — jumped a lorry part of the way. Some cooks at Edge Hill gave us tea and we learnt from a motorcyclist that the 41st Div. was at Ribemont, a few km further back. We jumped a train but it only took us a few yards. After waiting [threequarter] hour we decided to walk to Mericourt where the RTO [Railway Transport Officer] put us into a Rest Camp and promised us some breakfast.

26.9.16
Today I am posted to the 122nd Infantry Brigade, and Stace to the 124th Inf. Bde. We're taken up on a limber. Found the 122 encamped in tents and bivvies on the heights at Dernancourt overlooking Albert. Reported to the Signal Officer who seems pretty supercilious. His name is Buchanan. I'm in amongst a crowd of Scotsmen from the wilds of Glasgow and they don't exactly open their arms and embrace me.

27.9.16–1.10.16
These few days I have done nothing in particular except run messages and have two journeys to the baths at Méaulte. We have to walk about a mile each day to get an ordinary wash in the River Ancre. Talked to a German prisoner who is confident that the Germans will win in the end.

2.10.16

Up early and dismantled the camp. About 9 a.m. we moved off to go up the line. Since I left England the weather has been fine, but today it started to rain about 11 a.m. and it continued to pour throughout the march. We were soon wet to the skin, the water trickled down our bodies and into our boots. We arrived at the remains of Mametz Wood, all trenches and shell holes and mud, and after erecting tents for the officers were given bivvy sheets and left to make ourselves comfortable. Hetherington, Bennett and I selected an excavation where Fritz had started to make a dugout, put branches across it and spread over the bivvy. Then we collected the driest wood we could find, lit a fire close to the entrance to our 'home', took off our clothes and dried them one by one as much as we could, tipped the water out of our boots, wrapped ourselves up and went to sleep. At 2.30 a.m. I was called to go on wagon guard for half an hour, during which time I wrote one or two letters huddled up under a tarpaulin.

3.10.16

The rain had ceased when we got up but the roadways are swimming in liquid mud. They look nice and level but really they are full of big holes, and although usually the mud is not above the ankles yet every now and then you go in up to the knee. Horses and mules fall down every few yards. After a few miles of this we left the road and went along a track over open country.

The going soon proved too heavy for the mules, and also we were getting into the danger region so we unloaded the limber, each man taking as much as he could carry — the rest we left to be fetched later on. So we went across country, worming our way between guns of all sorts and sizes till we came to a trench called Fish Alley. Down this we went a long way to Ferret Trench which was our destination. The Signal Office and Officers' Quarters were down a deep dugout. Our billet was an old German dugout, dug in the face of a high bank, and, of course, facing the line. The village of Flers is close by and a crippled, battered tank, one of the first used in war, is lying almost opposite. Field batteries are all round us and this seems a pretty warm shop. Our dugout is filthy — lice and flies by the million and the stench of dead bodies makes one sick. One of our orderlies started to dig a hole in the bank to put his equipment in and came across a boot. He pulled it and a leg came with it.

4.10.16
This morning I was the first one up and went outside to get a breath of comparatively fresh air. Found Macdougall, the acting cook, astir, but he had no water. I offered to try to get some. There are wells in Flers but Fritz has got the range of each one. Although the journey was only a few hundred yards it took some time, dodging shell holes and bits of trenches and gun emplacements. Two RFA [Royal Field Artillery] men

arrived at the well at the same time as I did, fortunately, for it was three men's work to get the water up. The winch was broken and we lowered our petrol cans by means of a length of telephone wire. It took a long time to fill up, meanwhile Fritz was getting busy and we had only just got away when he began to drop 'em all round the well. While I was gone the Sergeant (Twycross) came round and found out what had happened. He stormed and raved and cursed Macdougall for letting a man go singly to such a spot but I got back safely with the two petrol cans of water and so we had some tea, which otherwise we might have whistled for.

5.10.16 and 6.10.16

The Signal Officer, who hasn't taken very kindly to me, doesn't consider that I am capable of taking over regular duties in such a strenuous period, so I am on all sorts of odd jobs. Rations are scarce — we get only two meals a day each, consisting of a half-pint of tea, one or two biscuits and a piece of bully or a little jam. Some of us have been out on the scrounge; we found some cases of bully and biscuits and brought back as much as we could carry. The rations are brought up to the dump, a few hundred yards away, each night, but Fritz generally manages to blow some of them into the air. Ours went west one night but two men who were guarding them didn't get touched.

Spent some hours on the parapet this evening trying to get visual communication with the

Hants [Hampshire Regiment]. Raining all the time. All our pigeon baskets got blown to bits, but there were no birds in them and one shell landed right in our trench a few yards away from me and wrecked an Artillery Observation Post. One man (RFA) was wounded and buried, but he was got out all right. Another shell landed on top of an Artillery dugout close to ours and a young fellow came running and screaming up to us. He wasn't wounded but had been badly shaken so I took him along to where there had been a Dressing Station, but that had gone so I took him back along the trench and he was crying loudly all the time and calling out 'Oh my mother, oh my mother'. I could get nothing out of him and when I had got him back as far as Longueval I laid him on a truck to wait for an ambulance to pick him up. I could do no more.

I've had a most welcome parcel from Lil — never did good food taste so really good — but oh for a good drink of pure water. A pint of petrol-tainted tea a day is all we get. We have used the water from our bottles sparingly and guarded it almost savagely — so easily does the primal instinct of self-preservation rise above all the teaching and training of centuries of civilisation. Bennett and I went back a couple of miles risking shells and bullets all the way in the hope of filling our bottles. It was a journey in vain although some RFA men gave us a drink out of their scanty store. A big shell landed just outside our dugout and made a hole big enough to take a General Service wagon. Another blew up six dead Germans to add to the intolerable stench. You can hardly go ten yards in any direction without coming across dead bodies or parts of bodies — an arm here, and a leg there. In trying to cross a very muddy track I stepped on what appeared to be a white stone — it was a skull. Buchanan unbent far enough to ask me what I thought of modern warfare, I told him 'not much'.

7.10.16
All this morning Fritz continued his strafing but at 2.30 p.m. we launched an attack. Then he stopped shelling us and gave his attention to the front line. The infantry only got about 100 yards — in some places not so far. They got mown down by machine-gun fire. The attack was a failure. In the evening I had to go to Tock Esses (= TS = Test Station) with Southwood so that I may know the way as I may be wanted to guide some officers up there later on. Davidson, Carter, O'Brien and McLachlan were there. It was difficult going owing to the large numbers of wounded who were coming down.

8.10.16
I waited till 3 a.m. in the trench by the Signal Office but nobody came along so I was allowed to go to my billet. The shelling was not so bad this morning. Both sides seem tired after the exertions of yesterday. Early in the afternoon I managed to get a bit of a wash and a shave, the first I have had for six days. Then a number of us

were sent for and told to find our way to Carlton Trench. In addition to our overcoats and equipment we were loaded up with all manner of Signal Stores, so much so that my knees quavered under me. We split up in two or three groups — Dickson, Brady and I were together — we progressed in easy stages along Fish Alley stumbling along the duckboards, but the real trouble began when we got out into the open with nothing but mud and shell holes. In attempting to step across a bit of trench I slipped and fell; and it was some minutes before I could get up. I now know what exhaustion means. Passed by a dead body in a shell hole that must have been laid there for weeks — couldn't tell if it were British or German. A little further on we took off all our clobber and had a rest on an old parapet. Once at Carlton Trench we soon got rid of our excess luggage and scrounged round for somewhere to sleep. Dickson and I found a sandbag shelter roofed with corrugated iron and settled ourselves in it. We can sit up in it and that's all. The 123rd Brigade are here and we went to their cook and begged a mug of tea and a slice of bread and jam. Dickson had a couple of parcels this morning and we had a feed of cold sausages and cake. This is the largest amount of food I have had in any one day since we left Dernancourt. Just before dusk we were called out to unload a wagon that had come up the transport track. This is one of the tracks that cut across country just anywhere and have not been made up at all; consequently it is knee-deep in mud. Even by picking your steps carefully you can't avoid going in over your ankles. They put as many as fourteen horses on an ammunition wagon and even then the poor beasts collapse and can't get up — and, of course, the wagon standing still gradually sinks deeper and deeper into the mud. I was ankle-deep when I stood by the wagon. They dumped a heavy officer's valise on to my shoulders and it pushed me further into the mud — up to my knees in fact — and I couldn't move. They removed the valise and I pulled myself out and after considerable struggling managed to get away with my load. Later in the evening I was told off for duty as 'check' at the Staff Office. All I did was to hang about the trench shivering and hungry for three or four hours. The Officers' cookhouse was close by and the smell of roasting meat made me ravenous, but it is worse than sacrilege to go near the Officers' cookhouse except on business. One man noticed me and I suppose I looked gaunt and hungry for he offered to try and get me something to eat. Presently he came back with a hunk of bread which I fairly gobbled up. But it was a long way from being sufficient and when the cooks shut up the cookhouse and went to bed, temptation was too strong for me — I broke into that cookhouse and hacked off a great lump of roast beef with my jackknife, grabbed a lump of bread, shoved both into my pocket and then returned to my post. I ate all that meat, fat, gristle and everything, and felt all the better for it. I shall always feel a deep sympathy with the man who steals food because he is starving.

12.10.16
About four o'clock I woke up feeling very queer.
Got up and went outside but everything swam
round and round and I clutched hold of the
bivvy pole or I should have fallen. After a time I
crawled back and got a little more sleep. After
breakfast we marched down to the railhead,
which has been pushed up this far since we were
here ten days ago. We entrained and were taken
as far as Méaulte, where a small party of us were
immediately despatched to the old camping
ground at Dernancourt to erect tents and get
things ready for the others. I am sharing a bivvy
with Dickson and McCormack.

15.10.16
This morning the Divisional Commander
(General Lawford) reviewed the Brigade. Before
he turned up, General Towsey (our Brigadier)
said a few words to us about the recent stunt.
The 11th Royal West Kents were the only
battalion on the whole of the attacking front who
dug themselves in in advance of the original line,
but even this bit of trench was lost by the
battalion which relieved them. So much for that
victorious onslaught!

16.10.16
Up early, struck camp and marched to
Mericourt where, after waiting some hours, we
were packed into railway trucks — about
thirty-five or forty men in each truck — barely

33

room to stand. Made the usual steady progress and cheered ourselves by singing and making a great deal of noise. But after nightfall our spirits flagged and we wished to rest. We curled ourselves up as well as we could, legs and feet and heads and arms were all mixed up in a horrible jumble and every now and then there was a hearty cursing when somebody got another man's boot in his eye. It would have been impossible to tell which legs belonged to which head or which head was the owner of a certain pair of arms.

17.10.16
After travelling about twenty-five kms in eighteen hours we arrived at Oisemont just after dawn and then marched several miles to a chateau. I'm not very certain as to whereabouts we are but it's somewhere in the neighbourhood of Abbeville. Soon after leaving Oisemont it came on to rain and we got pretty wet. I was glad to dry my clothes at the transport cook's fire. Our billet is a sort of loft approached by a rickety ladder but the straw is a luxury after so much of mother earth, and also we have been issued with a blanket. We had them given to us when we got back to Dernancourt — and that was not before we needed them.

20.10.16
Up long before daybreak and started a long march by the light of the moon and without any

breakfast. It was very exhausting — twelve miles on an empty stomach, and carrying about 80lbs of equipment is a pretty stiff task. McCormack was pushing a bike and he offered to strap my rifle to it but I declined. About 9 a.m. we arrived at Longpré station where the cooks, who had come in advance with the transport, had prepared our breakfast, but before we could touch it we had to get the horses and mules and weapons loaded up. Then we moved off through Abbeville, Etaples, Boulogne, and St Omer to Caestre where we arrived after dark. The journey was considerably swifter than any other I have had in France. From Caestre we marched to Eecke where we were billeted in a big room with a large fireplace. I was among the last to get up the ladder and so lost a position against the walls and had to make up my bed with three or four others in the middle of the room where we ran a certain risk of being walked on.

21.10.16
Eecke is not a bad little village. The church is just opposite our billet and our Signal Office is in the Tower. Spent the afternoon in the billet writing letters. Frank Wallace came in rather the worse for liquor and started doing and saying silly things. When he began to be abusive to Sgt Oxley I thought it was time to clear out — wish I had done so sooner, for later on Buchanan met me and told me that I should be wanted to give evidence. Don't relish this at all. These Scotsmen don't like Oxley and if my evidence goes against

Wallace it will be all the harder for me to make friends with them. They are terribly clannish and don't take to strangers in the least. Had my hair cut by a woman barber.

24.10.16
After a short spell on wagon guard I took a short stroll through the military-infested village and was then put on guard over Frank Wallace. This duty lasted all night but, of course, prisoner and guard both had a good night's sleep. Our bed during this night was the uneven, badly worn brick floor of a brewery. With only a groundsheet to lie on it was the most uncomfortable bed I ever laid on, but nevertheless we slept.

25.10.16
Crossed the Franco-Belgian border east of Abeele. Into camp at Zevecoten, just outside Reninghelst. Took over from an Australian Brigade who left the huts very dirty. These huts are ancient, leaky buildings made of wood, roof felting and tar — they are practically all roof. The one I am in boasts a door. There are a number of beds, wooden frames with wire netting stretched across and supported by four legs, more or less rickety. My immediate neighbours are McCormack on my right and Dickson on my left. There are plenty of rats.

29.10.16

Had a brainwave — discovered a brilliant way to let Elsie know my whereabouts. Told her to get a *Daily Mail* Birdseye Map of the British Front and later in the letter gave an answer to a mythical problem in terms of figures which appear on the map. I think she will twig it all right. Andy McCormack has been on the scrounge and brought home a stove which we have rigged up and, although fuel is scarce, we have a fire each evening and generally one of us does some washing. I did some socks and handkerchiefs last night, but dispensed with the starching and ironing.

1.11.16

Had a lovely parcel from Elsie and there are some others on the way from Mother, Lil and Ada. Have managed to get a soft cap at last — been wearing a tin hat ever since we were on the Somme, as I put my soft one on the GS wagon when we went into action. The wagon got 'done in' and a lot of stores were lost including the mail, though parts of this arrived before we finally left Dernancourt.

The housing problem is an acute one for the civilian population for there are so many refugees who fled before the German onslaught in 1914 and have just taken what shelter they could find. Just outside Abbeville I saw a 'home' which was only a wretched wooden shed about eight feet square, certainly no more than ten. In this single room lived a woman and four children. The husband was at the front.

2.11.16

Steady downpour all day long. Weather is worse than we get in England. No wonder Uncle Toby in *Tristram Shandy* said 'our armies swore terribly in Flanders'. They had the same sort of weather and probably less comfort. Was on duty this afternoon and now (7 p.m.) the rain has ceased and the moon is shining brightly. My mug of water is boiling on the stove so I must make my Oxo and then get to bed.

4.11.16

Quite a fine day. This afternoon I sat outdoors and wrote letters. A parcel arrived from Mrs Berwick which she posted on 22 September, six weeks ago — but the grub was all good — also a parcel from Ada. Sergeant Twycross is irreverently known as 'Callipers' owing to the shape of his legs.

5.11.16

Frank Wallace had his court martial and has no hope of acquittal. It's a crime to be drunk — there are no degrees of intoxication — you are either drunk or sober in the army. Evidence of your having had ½ a glass of watered beer is sufficient to prove that you were drunk and your punishment would be the same as if you had had a barrel and were right royally and nobly 'blind'.

6.11.16
Wallace was sentenced to two years' hard labour, but this was subsequently reduced to ninety days' Field Punishment No. 1. He has been returned to Division to undergo his sentence.

7.11.16
Vile weather. Haven't been outside my hut all day except to go to the Signal Office or to the cookhouse. Sent a parcel of odds and ends off to Mrs Berwick together with *A Girl of the Limberlost* for Elsie. I have made dots under a lot of letters commencing on p. 140 which when sorted out will provide interesting information of my doings.

8.11.16
Soon after breakfast we marched off to Dickebusch where our headquarters are at the burgomaster's farm. We came up through Ouderdom and right through the village of Dickebusch which is very much battered. It consists of one street with just a few outlying houses and a church. Every building is in ruins. Burgomaster's farm is in front of the village nearer to the line and is practically unharmed. The burgomaster and his wife, both old people, still live there although for over two years they have been in continual and very real danger. The Officers live in the farmhouse, all except Buchanan, and he has a dugout next to the Signal Office. This latter is a pretty strong

dugout camouflaged to represent a straw stack, but is generally known as the 'Haystack'. The men are accommodated in a number of small dugouts ranged along two sides of the field.

12.11.16
Well, this is the most comfortable billet I have struck since I left England, and so long as old Fritz keeps as quiet as he is at present I shall be able to stick this for a long while. The dugouts are old and frail and you can only stand up straight in certain places but we can make them warm and comparatively dry. The men who were in here last built a brick fireplace and we have got a home-made table and stools. It's a bit of a business to keep the fire going — we have to scrounge the wood, bring it in and chop it up. Yesterday I spent a lot of time wrestling with a young tree — broke a felling axe and gave myself a whack on the knee — it's a bit painful but we've got the wood. My letters are now coming with a rush. In the last two days I have had twelve letters and three parcels. My comrades in this dugout are Capt. J.C. Hamilton, Cpl Davidson and Andy McCormack. There is room for one or two more, so we are not overcrowded. Three of our men, Cpl Davidson, Jack Carter and John O'Brien, have been awarded the Military Medal for work done on the Somme. Have just heard a little incident that happened on the Somme. Tom McLaughlin was cooking some potatoes up at his Test Station and to get a better blaze he picked up what he thought was a rocket

dugout and the Haystack, missing the duckboards by a few inches. As the bits settled I made a dash for it and got into the Haystack dugout quite safely. Hamilton followed me and a 'five-nine', which landed a few yards from the door, caused him to come in head first without any ceremony. After this the shelling subsided. The mail came up later on and I had a parcel from Mrs Berwick which, after examining, I carefully tied up again, a very wise course for when I came off duty just after 5 p.m. it was so dark that I tripped over the duckboards and fell full length into the soft juicy mud. During the evening two RAMC men came to take away the body of the RE. Davidson and I helped them to get the body out of the dugout and on to a stretcher. The next day (9.1.17) Buchanan vacated his dugout. Ours had been a good bit shaken and we had been busy patching it up, but B sent word that we could have his old one. We didn't give anybody else a chance to get into it and started to move straightaway although it was pitch-dark. Our new home was absolutely bare, so we had to knock down our old beds and cart them away and re-erect them.

21.1.17
The weather is now very cold — 17 degrees of frost last night — the huts are white inside as well as out, but the ground is firm and hard and this weather is infinitely preferable to the rain and mud we have endured for so long.

25.1.17

The hard frost continues and, generally speaking, things are quiet from a warfare point of view. There are occasional raids by one side or the other at various parts of the line, but beyond a little shrapnel now and then Fritz leaves us alone. He pays more attention to the batteries which are all round us but not so close as to bring the enemy's attentions to our little corner. For this we offer up thanks.

31.1.17

Have had a little more snow. The ground is white everywhere and at night time it shows up a remarkable reflection from the Verey lights [flares fired from a pistol] although they are four or five miles away in a straight line. The signs of the times seem to point towards increased activity on this front in the spring. A great deal of work is being done in this neighbourhood in the way of dump-making and laying railway tracks. A broad-gauge track is being brought up right through Reninghelst to Ouderdom. Of course, nobody knows what it all means — we can only guess.

Have had some lively arguments lately regarding the termination of the war. It is interesting to notice how desires form into opinions. Quite a number of the fellows reckon on March or April seeing the end. I laugh at them and say '1929' but in serious argument I say that the war may last until 1920. So I am looked on as a miserable pessimist but despite all my hopes and desires I cannot imagine the war finishing this year. The people who are running the war are not doing any of the fighting!

6.2.17

Last night was a blighter — the thermometer has touched zero once or twice lately and last night it went below. I was on night duty in the Haystack (where we have a switchboard now that the Signal Office has been transferred to the Farm Cellar). Harvey Dale was the runner on duty with me and we shivered with cold all night long. A wood fire was impossible because there is no fireplace or stove and no ventilation other than the door. Charcoal was not to be got or we would have had a fire in the petrol-can brazier. So we just had to stamp about all night long. About 3 a.m. I got out my Tommy's Cooker, boiled up some water and made a pint of soup. This was very welcome but we could have done with a gallon. Cpl Cole (motorcyclist) has had his skates sent out and spends his spare time skating about the moat. Incidentally, the ice on the moat provides us with a short cut to the Farm. The other day a game of hockey was played on Dickebusch Lake. Fritz took no notice but the next day he put a few big shells into it.

9.2.17

Last night the Kents carried out a raid — the preliminary bombardment was very heavy and the raid was quite successful from a military point of view. A party of REs went over with them to do demolition work. I went on night duty in the Signal Office at 10 p.m. and about midnight twelve German prisoners were brought into the Brigade Offices. They were a mixed lot but most were fairly well built. The Brigade Major got a little information out of them — they were all jolly well fed up and glad that they had finished with the fighting, albeit a bit apprehensive as to their immediate fate. Subsequently they were taken by motor lorry back to Division.

While the raid was on I was busy taking messages — Buchanan and Ainger (Staff Capt.) and Reap (Intelligence Officer) were all in a state of excitement, particularly the latter two — Buchanan never shows much excitement. They came buzzing around me, causing me to get unnecessarily flurried. The messages were coming off in code and it's not an easy matter to receive when three or four officers are crowding round you watching each letter that you write and grabbing the form before you have finished writing. However, the man who was sending to me was a better operator than most and I got his messages correctly. But presently Buchanan came down and said, 'This is wrong, Martin, why don't you pay more attention to your work?' I looked at the message and replied, 'That's exactly as it was sent.' 'No it isn't,' he said, 'get it sent over again.' So I had to call them up and get them to repeat — it came through just as before — still Buchanan was not satisfied, so I had to get it repeated three times, and B went off in a huff. He hadn't been able to find fault with me. Later, after the prisoners had gone and the Brigadier and Brigade Major had retired, he sent for me to go up to the Officers' Mess, gave me a dose of rum and asked me if I knew anything about lighting fires. I said I had lit a few since I had been in France so he asked me (not ordered) to have a try at lighting his. So I obliged and then retired to the Signal Office. While I was lighting the fire, one of the Kents' officers came in and related sundry incidents that occurred during the raid. The Kents tried another raid later on but found Jerry ready for them and had to retire.

11.2.17

Buchanan gave me a fatherly lecture — says that the duties of a signaller demand resource and initiative, and that there are times when he must act on his own and not be bound by the rigidity of Army Rules and Regulations — he may be praised or he may 'get hell' for it, that just depends on how things turn out, but he's got to risk that. Also my demeanour is rather 'off-handish' and I continually appear to be thinking about things other than my work. I listened very attentively till he had finished, then said 'Very good, sir', saluted, turned round and gave myself a smile.

16.2.17

Been feeling very depressed and miserable so that for two whole days I refrained from writing any letters at all, but today I bought two green envelopes from one of the runners for a franc and have written a long letter to Elsie. It has done me good and I feel in better spirits. But oh, the utter desolation of this life out here. Absolutely helpless and impotent, we feel ourselves to be the wretched tools of an inexorable fate. It is bad for us to sit down and think — we become morbid. No wonder that the majority of the men, as soon as we get out of the line, turn their attention to estaminets and vin blanc.

18.2.17

Had a parcel, containing a nice lot of fruit from Mrs Berwick; also enclosed was a copy of a very painful pamphlet prophesying all sorts of terrible things about the war, and based on the books of Daniel and Revelation and on the movements of the sun, moon and planets. Quite amusing reading, especially as already a good many of the predictions have failed in fulfilment. Its chief point of interest, however, is in the prophecy that this war will last till 1929; then we shall have two years of peace, after which will break out a war more terrible and awful than this one, and it will be engineered and ordered by the present Crown Prince.

23.2.17
Didn't get any mail at all for three days and now it's coming in with a rush. I shall have a busy time answering them all. My watch is going all right but seems to have a pain inside it because it groans a bit when I wind it up.

1.3.17
A fine spring morning, and a blackbird came outside my dugout and sang just like the one that frequents the tall elm tree at the back of my house at Ealing, and used to wake me up with his whistling. This weather, the sweet spirit of spring swells in the hearts of men, and fills us with hopes and longings for something better than this sordid existence. In this way, perhaps, it makes us feel more discontented than we were in the very bad weather.

10.3.17
Snow yesterday, rain during the night and now the thermometer has made a big jump upward. Have done quite a lot of letter writing during this spell out of the line.

14.3.17
Wrote five letters, the first for several days as I have been in a very 'pippy' frame of mind. — I am thoroughly 'fed up and far from home'. The absurdity and utter imbecility of war only becomes more apparent the longer one is out here.

22.3.17
Woke up to find about two inches of snow on the ground. Then the sun came out and melted it but all day long we have been getting fierce blizzards of snow with biting cold winds, and in the intervals the sun has shone out of a deep blue sky flecked with a few white feathery clouds in regular spring fashion. According to the Almanac, spring started at 4.27 a.m. yesterday but tonight it doesn't feel very springlike. This evening I've been trying to warm up the hut, but as soon as the fire goes out it will be bitterly cold. My illumination is a solitary candle stuck on top of an empty rum jar and I'm sitting on the end of Colin Veitch's bed because that's the nearest point to the fire. Otherwise it is not a very comfortable seat as it is not joiner made and nails stick up in such profusion as to demand considerable care in sitting on it. Now I am going to pack up and get into bed for tomorrow we are off to Dickebusch again.

23.3.17
Arrived at Dickebusch safely. Had a parcel from Lil containing a body belt folded up just as she had bought it. When I unfolded it a piece of paper dropped out — I picked it up and read this:

Miss Dulcie Bennett
III Mansfield Road
Nottingham

Wishes the boy who receives this belt the best of luck and a safe return to Blighty. XXXX for luck

Oh, Dulcinea, I am no Don Quixote so I vulgarly displayed your missive to other eyes and there was quite a competition between several fellows as to who should have it and write to you. I even cruelly left them to settle the matter between themselves. But listen, Dulcie, one of these young men makes quite a profession of answering little notes of this sort and already he has a large collection of photos he has written to.

24.3.17
Fritz has been pretty quiet all this month but has gradually increased his activity till this evening he burst out ferociously. I was on 5–10 p.m. duty in the Signal Office. About 7 o/c a violent bombardment was going on on our front and Fritz was shelling all round us pretty liberally. When I came off duty at 10 p.m. the bombardment had slackened down almost to normal on the front line but Fritz kept plugging us with his heavy black shrapnel. He sends them over in threes with about two-minute intervals. I waited till one triplet had burst and the pieces settled, then made a bolt for my dugout which I reached only just in time to avoid the next issue. A West Kent private, by name W. Taylor, was buried up to his neck by a 'Minnie' [nickname for the *Minenwerfer*, or trench mortar]. A party of men were going to dig him out but he shouted

that he could stay where he was until the fire slackened. Eventually he was rescued uninjured. For this he was rewarded with the Military Medal.

28.3.17
Looking across the moat into the Farm Garden I noticed some crocuses in bloom. Called out all the dugout to see them and we nearly went barmy with excitement for they are the first flowers we have seen since we left Eecke on 25 October last.

1.4.17
Palm Sunday. The Belgians observe this day by taking big lumps of box tree to church.

Haven't seen any of the usual palm which graces this season in Blighty. Men, women and children were all carrying lumps of box down to the church this morning and looked quite serious over it. This plant grows into bushes and small trees out here — it is not trimmed down into a garden border as it used to be at home. I suppose it's the Belgian equivalent of the Judean Palm. The weather is not much like April, cold winds and blizzards of snow, so of course I've clicked for an outdoor job. Brady, Coultherd, McCormack and I have been told off for practice in signalling to aeroplanes. Each morning and afternoon we proceed with our 'flapper' [white-painted canvas used to signal] to an appointed spot in a field just off the Wesboutre Road. There we are joined by men from each of the battalions similarly equipped. Lieut. Walker (commonly known as 'Hookey' or 'Shugley') of the East Surreys is in charge. We adopt various methods of keeping ourselves comparatively warm until the 'Contact' aeroplane arrives when we can send and receive a few practice messages.

9.4.17
Originally there were only five of us in our dugout, but when two or three of the others started to collapse a few weeks ago we found shelter for two more, to wit, O'Brien and Robertson. Now we feel rather crowded but, of the seven, two of us are English and four are Scotch while O'Brien is cosmopolitan — Irish parentage, born in Glasgow, lived some time in London, and is very keen in argument, so keen, in fact, that he varies his nationality according to the turn of the argument. If anything good has been done by Scotsmen, he is a Scot, if by Irishmen, then he's Irish and the same with the English. If anything derogatory to one nation is mentioned, well, he belongs to one of the others. On Sundays, out of the line, he and Brady are Catholics because, being so few in number, they don't have Church Parade. Robertson is the baby of the section, both in years and appearance. He is round all over, round face, round body and round legs. Probably known as 'Fatty' in his schooldays. He and O'Brien are bosom pals and, as such, are constantly

quarrelling but it's fatal to take sides with either for then they immediately unite and present a solid front to the common enemy. Dagnall is the other Englishman — comes from Cheshire and is a foreman of Post Office linemen. He is grandfather of the dugout, I am father, the rest being children of twenty to twenty-four except McCormack, who is twenty-six and is affectionately styled Mrs McCormack because he acts as housekeeper and looks after the rations and performs all the maternal duties of the establishment. Aitken is the 'Cheese King' — has ideas of settling down in Cheddar after the war. He has toasted cheese for breakfast, dinner, tea and supper and frequently between meals, generally drops more into the fire than he succeeds in cooking. Also he is the most neatly groomed person in the section — seems to take a pride in his personal appearance — even cleans his boots and buttons and brushes his hair when there is no need for it at all. Frequently been known to wash twice in one day. Otherwise intelligent and a very decent fellow.

Davidson is the terror of the dugout and, indeed, of the whole section. A big, strong, fair-haired young giant with a voice, yes, yes, with a voice. Has got a lot of reserve energy which he endeavours to dispose of by vocal effort. When he discovered that I was musical he asked for my opinion on his voice. He was insistent but I remained polite for many days. At last I was driven to tell him that he was one of those blighters with music in his soul but precious little in his voice. Then I bolted, but he took it as a good joke, didn't feel ticked off in the least, and now he warbles away, more than ever. Repertoire very limited. Knows a lot of tunes but only a few words of each. This is how he sings one called 'The Five-Fifteen':

Lumpty-umpty-umpty-um five-fifteen
Lumpty-umpty-umpty-um five-fifteen
Lumpty-umpty-umpty-um five-fifteen
Lumpty-umpty-umpty-um five-fifteen.

O'Brien likes the words of this song so well that he usually calls for a second verse. Davidson starts to warble as soon as he wakes in the morning and is quite impervious to all threats, pleadings, cajoling and ridicule. I got so annoyed the other morning that I thought if he could be so cheerful it was really time he got up. But he wouldn't be persuaded and at last, greatly daring, I reached over and took hold of his nose very firmly and pulled; he came out of bed with a jerk. I didn't know that he had a terribly sore nose, but he wouldn't accept any apologies, so, out of bed I came, blankets and all and was rolled on the floor of the dugout. He is always the last to get to bed and keeps lullabying from about 10 till midnight, but nothing short of absolute destruction will keep him quiet — sleep only brings a change of utterance, for no matter how often we wake during the night, Davidson is yap-yap-yapping away about something or somebody. The only gratifying aspect of it is that he doesn't sing in his sleep. And he is going to get married after the war! Poor wee wife!

10.4.17

We are having a very busy turn in the line again. In the ordinary course I should only have been on duty for four hours today but I was operating the telephone switchboard from 8 a.m. to 10 p.m. with only brief reliefs for dinner and tea. Had a beat-up with an officer. Oh how cocky and important some of these creatures become as soon as they get into officers' uniforms! Lieut. Hogg, the Divisional Observation Officer, called me up and asked for one of his Observation Posts so I put him through without any trouble, but when he had finished he called me up and let drive without any warning. Said that he had been calling for ten minutes before he got an answer. I told him I answered directly he called. He cursed and swore and called me a liar and sundry other nice kind names, took my name and number and said he would report me to the Staff Captain and see that I got properly punished. When he had finished I got hold of Sgt Twycross and told him my version. I didn't fear much because this is the sort of affair in which Buchanan will stand by me. He may strafe me himself but he won't let Staff Captains or Divisional OOs or anybody else interfere with his section. However, there was no need to trouble at all for only a few minutes later Hogg called me up again and made a really handsome apology saying that the trouble was due to a loose wire at his end which resulted in only intermittent connection. So now I can sleep in peace. Later in the evening he came into the Haystack for no apparent reason at all, was very nice and affable and gave me a cigarette. Suppose he only wanted to see who I was.

13.4.17
Back to Reninghelst. We had just got settled in and had tea when there was the sound of a shell burst. This was most extraordinary as Fritz has never dropped any shells in this neighbourhood. We all rushed out of our huts to see what was up when there was a terrific whizz and a thud and lumps of dirt and mud flew up all over us. A shell had pitched close to the door of the Officers' Kitchen only a few yards from where we were standing. The Brigade Major came out and ordered us to disperse, so we cleared off in all directions but we saw another shell burst behind the Post Office Hut and one in the direction of the Ouderdom Dump. The shelling was only a spasm, however, and soon everything was normal again.

14.4.17
Some Artillery Officers have been up to examine the shell hole. It turns out that although it landed with a deuce of a roar it didn't explode. If it had done it would have accounted for the best part of Brigade HQ. Fortunately it struck a deep bed of soft mud which was insufficient to explode it. The hole at the top is about four or five feet across and about five feet down it becomes just a hole twelve or fifteen inches in diameter. We probed this hole with long poles

but couldn't touch the bottom. The Artillery Officers say that it is an armour-piercing shell from a long-range high-velocity naval gun firing probably from a distance of fifteen miles. They would like to have dug up the shell; but that would take a battalion of men about a week. It was jolly lucky that it struck that very soft patch instead of coming a few feet further on and striking the comparatively hard surface of the lane. However, the powers that be have gained certain information as to the direction and distance from which the gun is firing.

15.4.17
We hear that our aeroplanes have spotted Fritz's long-range gun and they or our artillery have put it out of action. It was fifteen miles away from us and right on the other side of the sector. Very glad to know it's knocked out as we had thought it very unkind of old Fritz, after giving us a very lively time in the line, not to leave us alone when we got out here. Went down and had a look at the shell hole by the Post Office. It's a big one, almost as big as the one outside our dugout on the Somme. It fairly put the wind up Smithey and Peter Kenny, who, although they have been out here since 1914, have always been in safe places. This is about the first shell they have seen burst.

16.4.17

Heard a humorous tale about Sgt Maton, Brigade Vet. Sgt. He wrote a letter which somehow or other fell into the hands of some of the men in his hut. Being short of news he drew on his imagination and gave an extraordinarily detailed account of how, for the past six weeks, he and his comrades had been building themselves a dugout under terrific shellfire and he enlarged on the danger of his ordinary duties by telling how he had crawled into no-man's-land to minister to a wounded horse! And three days ago he had never seen a shell burst except 'Archies' [anti-aircraft fire]. This romancing is rather common amongst certain types of men. One fellow thought it a great joke when he told his parents that he had saved his Sgt Major's life and had been rewarded with a packet of fags. This same man went a bit further and told them that when he went over the top he came to a German dugout. He looked in and was greeted immediately with cries of 'Kamerade'. 'All right,' he said, 'come out, you blighters', and out trooped a hundred and fifty of them. He was taking them back when he met an officer who took charge of the party and subsequently laid claim to having captured them himself, but the man protested and the result was that neither of them got the VC!

17.4.17

In these huts I am not associated with the same bedmates as at Dickebusch. There are only five of us in this hut and we get all the disadvantages of open-air treatment without any of its compensations. Charlie Werry is another youngster something like Robertson — round all over — and he's infernally lazy but very cheerful withal; therefore he is one of those persons one gets on with very well, but would like to kick or turn out of bed and shake. It's very hard to rouse him to a sense of his responsibility for the care and cleanliness of the hut but on the rare occasions when he does wake up he will chop wood till the perspiration is trickling all down his body and oozing out of his boots. This is good for him, keeps him fit, so once started, we encourage him to keep on at it. His home is at Chichester. Colin Veitch is a canny Scot from Fife and was in Egypt and Gallipoli before he came to France. He bustles about and cleans up and generally acts a mother, always keeping an eye on the rations and the fuel and estimating if they will last us till the next issue is due. Dickson has several elder sisters but no brothers, therefore it's taking him a long time to get over the fondling and attention to which he was accustomed in civilian life. He is one of those blithe spirits who has never been known to smile and if he is a little out of sorts, dwells on the hardness of his lot a bit too much. He is the parcel specialist of the section. Nobody has been able accurately to reckon up how many parcels he gets in a month, but what with all his sisters, his parents and sundry other fond relations who think the poor lad is suffering untold privations and must be fed bountifully from home, there are times when he gets parcels nearly every day.

In this respect, of course, he is a desirable acquisition to our hut.

Hetherington, a North Countryman, is one of those rare geniuses who only once in a thousand years flash through the pages of history with the brilliance of a mighty meteor on a moonless night. He is a musician of no mean order and an artist who scorns to exhibit his paintings to the criticising and unappreciative public. So all these treasures he has locked away to be seen by no mortal eye until he returns to Blighty. His knowledge and grasp of social economics and politics are something beyond the ken of ordinary mortals; and time out of number he has addressed audiences of thousands and swayed them backwards and forwards by his incomparable eloquence, and has played on their emotions with the same skill and effect as he plays on the violin. There are a lot of other things at which he excels, indeed it is impossible for him to make a bungle of anything; and whatever he attempts he excels at immediately with that ease and grace which cannot be acquired but which are natural to him. Remarkable, but nevertheless true, because he keeps on telling us so. Incidentally, he is the section's appetite and if ever there is a mysterious shortage of grub we know where to lay the blame. One day I saw him eat a one pound tin of jam straight off in about three gulps.

A few weeks ago I was down by Reninghelst church when I saw a rural Belgian funeral. Apparently it was the funeral of an elderly man, and his widow and grown-up children were the mourners. The hearse was a farm wagon (not much like a modern English one, more like those in Constable's pictures) drawn by two heavy draught horses, well-groomed and fitted with well-polished harness. This feature was noteworthy because ordinarily the Belgians don't give much attention to 'poshing up' their horses and harness. Over the wagon was the coffin together with two or three chairs occupied by the bereaved daughters. But the widow had the seat of honour in front of the wagon, low down, almost on the shafts and just behind the horses' tails. From this position she directed all the operations with just that amount of regal dignity which was appropriate to the occasion. The Belgians spitting here there and everywhere is not very pleasant especially when you see the women spitting on the floor and rubbing it out with their boots or wooden clogs, or the men doing it and the women running round mopping it up after them. I have an idea that social position goes by the number of times a man can spit in the same place. If he can make a cross without once misfiring he becomes a councillor and the man who can weave the most intricate pattern is made a burgomaster.

Back in January I was getting fed up with the army baths and, as I had collected three changes of fairly decent underclothing, I looked out for a chance of getting a private bath somewhere or other where I could have a good scrub down and leave my dirty clothes to be washed. I went up the La Clytte Road and crossed the fields to a little group of cottages where I found one with an 'Authorised to wash for Soldiers' notice in the window. An old lady answered my knock. 'Good morning, Madame, can you let me have a bath?' 'No compree,' she replied. I discovered that I had struck one of the few Belgians who couldn't speak any English. I don't know any Flemish so I tried 'Lavez?' — 'No compree' — 'Bathez?' 'No compree.' I began to get rather desperate so I rubbed my hands over my body and made various other antics intended to resemble a person having a bath, and then threw out my last word, 'Washez?' — 'Ja, Ja,' she replied, and her wrinkled features brightened up with intelligent comprehension. I sat down in the kitchen while she made the water hot in a great big kettle and prepared the ablution chamber. This chamber is a shed at the back of the cottage. The bath is a round wooden washing tub. I have a pailful of hot water and ditto of cold. The old dame provides a chair and I take my own time over my ablutions. When finished, I hand over my dirty clothes and get back the lot I left for washing on the previous occasion.

The woman does a lot of washing but has some system of marking so that she always brings out the right set. Only once have I had any trouble, and that was over a pair of socks — I got the wrong ones, but she soon put that little matter right. She knows me as 'Telefon' because my blue and white armlet declares me to be a Signaller.

All this winter we have realised that we have had a quiet time. Both sides have been quite content to hold on just where they were — and except for occasional raids into each other's territory, and a few artillery strafes just by way of keeping things from going to sleep altogether, we have not done much more than play at war. But things have livened up considerably during the last four or five weeks and we look forward to spring with very mixed feelings. It is evident that the Big Push is going to take place somewhere in this sector, but when and how and by whom are matters that lie in the laps of the gods. Many rumours are current but I have had so much experience of the birth and growth of rumours since I've been out here that I don't pay much attention to them. Yet I think it is pretty well settled that we are to go out for our long overdue rest. The 124th Brigade has had one and the 123rd are now having theirs in the St Omer region. Whether we are coming back to this neighbourhood to take part in the push, nobody knows.

In the camp just mentioned we passed a number of large wooden posts with ropes attached. This is where men, who are fighting for a country in which probably they have no interest except that Fate ordained that they should be born there, are tied up like slaves for two hours a day and in other ways punished for all sorts of trivial offences. Prussianism is not confined to the Germans. Our own military system is out and out Prussianism. I suppose the only way to persuade men to face the horrors and vileness of war is to drive them at the point of the bayonet, and mete out to them all manner of cruel punishments, holding over their heads the murderous threat of being shot at dawn. Such is the fierce, brutal discipline under which we live. The 'is and is not' of the King's Regulations and the various Army Acts are very definite and are interpreted in the most rigid Roman fashion — and of course the host of young schoolboys, clerks, counterjumpers and the like who have managed to fall into commissions, like to exert the authority reposed in them. Never having been in the position to order or command, and suddenly finding themselves possessed of power over their fellow men, they become snobs and tyrants of the worst description. Fortunately for us, Buchanan is not one of this class. Although for some reason or other he hasn't taken kindly to me yet, I must admit that he is a good officer: he looks after his men and he knows his work, and the best thing about him is that he won't let anybody else interfere with us.

23.4.17
A Corporal Flynn and two Signallers of the 23rd Middlesex have been left behind by the 123rd Brigade to instruct us in the use of the new portable directional Wireless Set. This morning we established two stations and got through several messages, but I can see there is going to be more holiday about this course than serious business. Flynn says this Wireless Set is the only one of its kind in France at present — it is a big advance on anything similar, the chief novelty being the use of 'valves', little bulbs like

incandescent electric light bulbs but containing wires other than the filament.

Mulligan was billeted in a cottage near the village with a couple of MPs [Military Policemen]. They had a bare room, and slept on the floor. M. discovered a spare bedroom in the farm and got permission to take it. It's a small room with a single bedstead, dressing table etc and family photographs on the walls. All very nice and comfy. I helped him get his kit down there and the farm girls asked me if I were the Sergeants' domestique! We had some coffee and sat talking for about [threequarter] of an hour when we decided it was time to get back to our posts previous to packing up for dinner. In the afternoon we had a lamp-reading test which was quite easy but John O'Brien cursed it — said he was an instrument repairer not an operator — so I read for him as well as myself but he thought it advisable to put a few extra mistakes of his own so as to avoid suspicion. Heard the cuckoo for the first time this year.

In the evening Horace (a Kent Signaller, don't know his other name) and I took a walk into the forest. We went along the road past a number of cottages when suddenly we met some Germans. It gave us a bit of a start because we thought we had left them a long way behind. It turned out they are prisoners located in a cottage right on the edge of the forest — a much better billet than we have got. They are guarded by a few French soldiers and are employed in tree-felling. The forest is on a hill and we climbed up through it till we reached a road — went along this for half a mile or so and then turned back into the forest and soon lost our bearings — climbed up a tree to get a look over the countryside and so found the direction to take. The other fellows laughed when we told them we had seen the wily Hun — they won't believe us.

24.4.17
A little more wireless — also coffee — this morning, and this afternoon 'visual'. I was in charge of one station with the three Surreymen. Going to take up our position, I noticed a hen sitting in the ditch. Said nothing, but later I heard a clucking, went back and discovered four eggs which, in accordance with the best traditions of the service, I promptly commandeered. We had one each for tea. This evening I was taking a quiet stroll when I saw Glasspoole and Cheesman going across the fields obviously on the track of the Hun, so I hailed them and conducted them to the cottage where some of the prisoners were just returning from their day's work and others were busy in the garden. So now, they believe us.

27.4.17
This week has been the easiest one I have spent in the army. It has been a regular holiday. Walker has troubled us but very little — about ten

minutes a day on average. Twice we have had a lecture on wireless in the village schoolroom. It was a job to squeeze into the little desks but we managed it. The walls are decorated with the same sort of pictures of birds and animals and scriptural subjects as those at home except that the Bible pictures here have a flavour of Catholicism. Each evening I have been down to the farm and had coffee. Lucienne speaks a little English and I speak less French so we get on all right. Two or three times I have bought eggs there and they have boiled them hard for me so that I could bring them back and eat them for supper. The family at the farm consists of the farmer, his wife, Lucienne (their eldest daughter, about eighteen) another daughter about fourteen, and a miscellaneous assortment of small children.

29.4.17
Now that I am so far from the line, in a spot where the heavy guns can only be heard when the wind is in the right direction, where there is no sign of war, and where the rural occupations of peacetime plod steadily along as if totally unconscious of the awful horrors that are taking place only a few leagues away, I feel my old love for the countryside reviving. I was half afraid it was dead, killed by spending so many months in about the most monotonous and soul-destroying region imaginable. It may be quite passable in peacetime, but war annihilates everything. Devastation and suffering are forced into one's

mind and with these things uppermost it is almost impossible to appreciate nature even in her most glorious moods. Now I am longing for Blighty — but oh, the heaviness of longing and waiting! I grow impatient and rebellious at times — although I know perfectly well that it is all to no purpose for we are very much the creatures of circumstance — paltry pieces on 'this chequer board of nights and days'. I slept this morning but got up for dinner, then did some writing but was interrupted with the call for Church Parade. This caused a bit of excitement as it is the first one we have had since the middle of October — the weather today is glorious — just as it was on this particular Sunday five months ago. The sun is bright and warm though there is a little chilliness in the wind and the birds are singing gaily.

2.5.17
Spring has burst upon us quite suddenly. Cuckoos, swallows, primrose, butterflies all seem to have come with a rush, and last night I heard the nightingale. I have just written seven letters, and am sitting on a big stone in the farmyard with my back against the wall. The sun is going down and a cuckoo is calling in the distance. Everything is absolutely peaceful. The only sign of war is an anti-aircraft gun which stands in the roadway close to the Signal Office — it comes up on a lorry every morning and goes away in the evening. It is manned by artillerymen who are suffering from nerves or who are otherwise

temporarily unfit for the strenuous life of active warfare up the line. Another sign of spring — a bee has just come buzzing round my head.

6.5.17
A 'rest' in the army does not mean the same thing as it does in civilian life. It really means a change of occupation: instead of fighting, we have innumerable parades, inspections, route marches, field days and the like — anything to prevent us from idling half an hour away. We have a continual round of duties so that I get precious little time for letter writing or reading.

12.5.17
Thank heaven we are having things a bit easier today. The last four days have knocked the stuffing out of me, particularly yesterday when it was very hot and we had a full dress rehearsal of the attack we are going to make when we get back in the line. I was at an advanced Signal Station when Buchanan came up and asked if anybody had any tobacco. I offered him my pouch and said, 'It is only Waverley' — 'Well, what's the matter with that?' he asked. I nearly said, 'Oh it's only boys' tobacco', but changed my mind and said, 'It's not very strong.' When he had gone, MacDougall told me that Waverley is B's favourite tobacco. Glad I changed my mind.

13.5.17

Buchanan had us all out (including the 'Forward Party') and gave us a little lecture on what is going to happen. We are going back to our old sector to make a big attack. The 123rd and 124th Brigades are going over first — we follow and take over from them on the Damstrasse then push on the final objective — presuming, of course, that Jerry doesn't protest too vigorously. We don't look forward to it with any particular joy.

Just south-east of the city of Ypres was the strategically important Messines Ridge. This naturally important position dominated the landscape and had been in German hands since the early fighting around Ypres in October and November 1914. Since then, the British had not seriously contested the strongpoint in the German line. However, since mid-1916 plans had been undertaken to take the ridge by literally blowing the enemy off it. In great secrecy, twenty-one mines would be dug underneath the German lines and exploded simultaneously. Those Germans left alive — indeed any who still retained any faculty for thought — would be assailed by infantry supported by artillery, tanks and gas.

The work to dig the mines took over a year and involved thousands of men not only to dig the tunnels but also to remove the vast amount of spoil. In the end eight kilometres of tunnels were dug; at the end of each were laid explosives that cumulatively weighed 600 tons. Only one of the twenty-one mines was discovered; the other twenty were primed to go. Then, at 3.10 a.m. on 7 June, the mines were detonated; only two failed to explode. The explosion could be heard in London, while on the ridge the Germans were not only stunned but stupefied, 10,000 being killed in the opening moments of the battle. The British forces advanced and in the main suffered relatively few casualties for the significance of the prize. German counter-attacks could only be organised the following day and failed entirely.

31.5.17
After seven weeks I am back in Dickebusch once again but the aspect of the country has changed. It is crowded with gunpits. Gordon Farm, which lies on the other side of Dickebusch Lake and a little nearer the line, has been inhabited by civilians until a few days ago. It has also been the HQ of an artillery brigade. The civilians were removed on account of the impending attack and within three days of their leaving Fritz had set fire to the place and razed it to the ground. It is now only a smouldering pile of rubbish and ammunition dumps. The derelict, waterlogged dugouts round the lake have been restored and now house one of our battalions. There is much more bite and sting in the shellfire and it is not safe to wander about as we used to do.

5.6.17

We are now at the Micmac Camp — came here this afternoon — the few days we spent at Dickebusch were not exactly pleasant, for Jerry is giving all his attention to the back areas, and the actual front line is peaceful. Our bombardment has been continual and terrific beyond imagination, and against it Fritz's retaliation, though pretty hot, can only be described as a bit troublesome. Once on the night of 29–30 May I was on night duty in the Haystack, Southwood was the runner with me. About 11 o/c I heard a Boche aeroplane flying about. This is the first time I have actually heard any night-flying although I have heard of it, even as long ago as last October on the Somme, when we had returned from the trenches and made up a big camp fire and had a 'sing-song'. We were advised to put it out as only a night or two previously the Hun had been over dropping bombs. I looked outside the Haystack and although it was bright moonlight I could see nothing. Later, about midnight, Southwood had fallen asleep on the doorstep, when I heard a shell fall a little nearer than is comfortable. It didn't make much of a noise and I concluded it was a dud. But it was quickly followed by another and another and then lots more all of the same score. Gas shells explode with a gentle 'plop' just like a dud 'five-nine' [5.9-inch shell] (that's why Fritz mixes them). So I sniffed the air and there was no doubt about it. I woke Southwood, told him to go round and warn all the dugouts, phoned through to the Signal Office and told them

— looked round for my gas mask and found I had left it in my dugout — the first time I have ever done it — so I rushed out to get it. The gas shells were now coming over in a continual shower, and with my hand over my mouth and nose I ran to the dugout, alarmed them all and got my mask on and returned to my post. It was a rotten business working a telephone switchboard with a gas helmet on. As much as possible I 'buzzed' but every now and then I had to loosen my mask and talk and then the gas got into my throat and made my eyes water terribly. After two or three hours of it Jamieson came running into the Haystack saying that his dugout had been hit, but fortunately no one was hurt. As these dugouts are such frail structures the men soon came trooping down to the greater security of the Haystack. There was one terrific explosion which nearly shook the dugout down on top of us. The candle was blown out and the place fairly rocked. We thought a shell had struck the top of the dugout but later we learnt that it was a 'toffee-apple' dump [two-inch mortars shaped like a ball on a stick] blown up on the other side of the lake. Fritz kept on with his gas shells and a few heavies until daylight.

6.6.17
This afternoon we were all ordered to pack everything in our valises, except fighting kit, and hand them to the care of the QM [Quarter Master]. At 6 p.m. L/Cpl Aitken, L/Cpl Dagnall,

100

Coultherd, Brady, MacDougall, Paterson, Robertson and I joined the Forward Party and moved up the line. We went by a newly made cavalry track, skirting Dickebusch on the north, and so past Scottish Wood into the trenches. In the shelter of some trees were a number of tanks in readiness for the attack. It was 9 p.m. before we were in our allotted positions in the support trenches. The front line trenches were manned by the 123rd and 124th Brigades. It was a wretched night — the strain of waiting was great — our guns were going continually — Fritz was 'nervy' and in addition to throwing over trench mortars and the like, kept his guns traversing our trench all the time. He had got it taped to a nicety and as the trench was so crowded there were a good many casualties. We (the Forward Party) had twelve men wounded, one having his left arm blown off — but none of the REs were hurt although for a few seconds I was given up for lost. I was crouched down in the trench with my back to Jerry when a small shell landed almost on the parapet a matter of only inches from my head. The trench came in on top of me and, but for the fact that it was strongly revetted, I should have been completely buried. When the smoke and dirt had cleared away, the other fellows were surprised to see me pick myself up unhurt. Aitken said, 'That one had got your name on it, Joe.' 'Yes,' I replied, 'but it was the wrong number.' It gave me a terrible shaking but it might have been much worse.

7.6.17

The night wore on with a miserable slowness but towards dawn the fire on both sides slackened and just before 3 a.m. we were ordered to leave the trench and lie out in the open. It was an impressive time — the gunfire ceased altogether with the exception of an occasional shell here and there — a thick mist was over the land and we had to lie full length, partly because of the shock that would result from the explosion of the mines and partly to prevent Fritz seeing us in the growing dawn. There was a strange groaning and rumbling from behind us and presently, looming out of the mist, came a tank, moving straight towards us. We began to scramble out of its way, but it turned off to the left and was soon buried again in the mist. Out of the silence came the sound of blackbirds from a clump of battered trees a little way back only to be rudely silenced at 3.10 a.m. by the tumultuous explosion of nineteen mines. This will probably be accounted as the greatest artificial explosion in recorded history. For several minutes the earth rocked to and fro oscillating quite twelve inches. It was an experience which I shall remember very vividly for the rest of my life — all the phases of the preliminary bombardment, the calm silence that succeeded them suddenly broken by a most terrific uproar, the weird sights of moving men and things in the semi-darkness, the rolling clouds of smoke picked out every now and then with shooting tongues of flame, all formed a tremendously wonderful sight. It was stupendous beyond the imagination.

The blowing up of the mines was the signal for all the guns on the front to open out. The noise rendered talking or shouting impossible. Every type of gun was in action, from immense howitzers to machine guns which were arrayed some little distance behind us and carried out a barrage all on their own. A few minutes later the 123rd and 124th Brigades went over and we returned to the trench. As daylight increased I looked directly on to the line that was being battered and the sight was so awfully impressive that the real horror of it all was temporarily quite obliterated. On our left, Fritz was sending over cloud gas — he also had an observation balloon up but this was soon put out of action by our aeroplanes. The prisoners came over in dozens and scores and passed behind us into safety. About 5 o/c 'Hookey' Walker took us out of the trench and we advanced to the Damstrasse. Ordinarily he has a languid sort of bearing that would give one the impression that he was rather dull and unobservant but he led us across that open, shell-holed country that only two hours before had been held by the Germans since 1914 as if he knew every inch of the ground. He didn't hesitate for a moment and took us straight to the dugout in which the 124th Brigade Advance Signals had established themselves. The Damstrasse is 1200 yards in front of, and overlooking, our old front line. It is a sunken roadway about six to eight feet lower than the surrounding country and therefore of considerable military advantage. At times we have imagined that Fritz has given us a tidy battering, but judging from the frightfully mutilated state of the ground, we have given him ten times as much as he has given us. His front line has been completely wiped out and is only traceable by the remains of his barbed wire, and it was only possible to find little bits of any trench.

As we went over, we passed through only a moderate barrage and met with no casualties although the dead bodies that were scattered about showed that other parties had not been so fortunate. When we reached the Damstrasse, however, we were fairly in amongst the shells for this was now our front line and Fritz was concentrating all his efforts in the attempt to prevent us from getting any further. Also many of our own guns were firing short, and spiteful 18-pdr [pounder] shrapnel was bursting all round us. The western bank of the Damstrasse was lined with dugouts, now in various stages of demolition. The one chosen for our Signal Office was fairly sound, being constructed of reinforced concrete about three foot thick. Lt Walker and Cpl Aitken went in to take over, leaving us outside in the remains of a trench which was labelled 'Engel Weg'. Col. Carey-Barnard (known as Carey-Whizzbang by reason of his rather explosive nature) came along leading the 15th Hants. Of course he wanted to know who we were, what we were, and all about us. The trench was rather cramped so we moved across to the east bank of the Damstrasse. Looking over the top, no Germans were visible but we knew they were lurking in shell holes and hiding in Ravine Wood and Pheasant Wood, both of which were only a few yards away.

We sat down on the bank waiting for orders and wishing to goodness that our 18-pdrs would lengthen their range. On my right was Dagnall and next to him was Coultherd. One of our 18-pdr shrapnels burst about six yards above our heads and the bits came hissing down viciously. I wasn't touched but Dagnall got it in both knees and Coultherd in the left knee. We ripped their breeches open and bandaged them up. I used my own field service dressing on Dagnall and subsequently got into trouble for being in action without one in my possession. We carried them across the road to the dugout where they remained till 8 p.m. before we got hold of any stretcher-bearers. It was about 5.30 a.m. when they were wounded. The Damstrasse is a slough — mud, water and shell holes. A shell burst right on top of the Signal Office and we went over expecting to find the place blown in but it was quite unharmed inside — evidence that Fritz knows how to build dugouts.

Presently the tanks came along. They had to drop down the bank about six or eight feet, wallow through the mud and climb the opposite bank. One came over the top of the Signal Office and again we feared for the safety of those inside but there was no need to worry. Another got stuck in the mud and refused to budge. At 6.30 a.m. the advance was continued for another 1000 yards to the final objective of the Division, the attacking battalions of our Brigade being the 15th Hants and the 11th Royal West Kents. There was not much opposition except from a machine-gun nest in Pheasant Wood. The bullets came 'zipping' over our heads until the Kents stormed it at the point of the bayonet. The Signal Office was small, and with two wounded men in it and one end under water, there was only room for one operator at a time; yet at certain periods it was necessary to have two instruments working, so I took a buzzer outside and rigged it up on a mound where the trench had been blown in. The dirt gradually wore away and disclosed the bare buttocks of a dead man so I moved into the Damstrasse where the only comparatively dry spot was alongside a dead German but he was not badly mutilated. An infantryman close by me was hit in the face by a quantity of shrapnel dust and his tears trickled down his cheeks. He cried out, 'Oh my eyes, my eyes! My God, I am blind!' The sudden realisation of his blindness seemed a greater agony than the pain of his wounds. I shall never forget that terrible cry of anguish. A big German prisoner passed me with his left arm badly shattered. He begged a drink of water but I shook my head because I had only a little drop left and had no idea when I should get any more. Two other prisoners came over, one unhurt, the other wounded in the arm and side. The former scrambled up the bank leaving his wounded comrade to struggle alone. There was a yell of execration from all the Tommies round about and it put the wind up him. He threw his hands up above his head and yelled 'Kamarade', and we made him go and help his companion along.

Time passed very slowly — I looked at my

watch, thinking it was afternoon and found it was only twenty past eight. I took off a message from the Kents saying that the Huns (500 of them) were massing for a counter-attack. Walker seized his revolver and went forth to meet them but soon came back as he had left his ammunition behind. This attack was repulsed by the Kents who killed twenty-five of the enemy and took twenty unwounded prisoners. We were due for relief at noon, but the relieving Division was delayed somewhere or other so we had to hang on, feeling very tired and hungry. Also we sent back several demands for cavalry as our advance had been so successful, but apparently the state of the country was such that rendered it impossible for cavalry to get up. The 47th Division on our left met a fiercer opposition and failed to take their final objective. Of course our 'lines' (telephone wires) were continually being broken — our stock of pigeons was soon exhausted — and our runners were on the go perpetually. In the afternoon I took a message forward to Lieut. Taylor. By this time things had quietened down considerably. I climbed up the bank and looked forward. With the exception of a solitary tank that had come to anchor just in front of me, there was no sign of humanity except that displayed by the general devastation, and the explosion of an occasional shell. My only guide was the 'line' which led me to a large shell hole in which Lieut. Taylor and his party had settled themselves. Fritz had ceased making any attempts at counter-attack and seemed to be content to settle down in his new position.

Lieut. Raphael, the Surrey cricketer, was up here this morning for no earthly reason as far as I can make out, other than that of souvenir hunting. He brought his batman with him and both were killed by a shell in a dugout which he was exploring. By the evening we had given up hopes of getting relieved today. Aitken and I settled down in the trench and tried to get a little sleep but Fritz started sending shells just over our heads to a spot about 200 or 300 yards away, and the shriek as they whizzed past was more than sufficient to keep us awake. He also treated us to some shrapnel — one burst just above us and a small piece hit me on the arm. It was long and thin and by a stroke of luck it struck me lengthways just where my sleeve happened to be rucked in several folds. If it had come end-on it would have gone through. I picked it up and put it in my pocket. It is the only souvenir I brought back although I could have had hundreds of belts, buckles, buttons, bayonets and such things as some men pride themselves in collecting. Outside the Signal Office was a great pile of arms and clothing together with black bread and sausages but although we were hungry we knew better than to touch any of it.

Towards nightfall Lieut. Taylor brought his men in and they found what shelter they could in the damaged dugouts nearby. We all had exhausted our supply of rations of any sort but I managed to get a drink out of a petrol can which two Hants men were taking up. I had brought a lump of bread with me but it had gone mouldy. The iron-ration biscuits are so hard that I had substituted this piece of bread and this was my reward. We were all dead beat and about 10 p.m. we crowded into the dugout to try and get some sleep. Yet one man had to be on duty so I offered to carry on till 3 a.m. when MacDougall would take over till 8 a.m. I was kept busy all the time for although things were quite quiet we were the only front-line Signal Office. Once I had to go out and find a runner and managed to slip into a shell hole of slimy mud and water. The poor wretch was, if possible, more worn out than I was but war is no respecter of weariness and I had to make him go on his journey. From the length of time he was away he must either have gone to sleep or have been too tired to find his way.

We captured a map on which it was clearly marked that Burgomasters Farm at Dickebusch was a Brigade HQ so that if Fritz had been so minded he could have blown us all to blazes at any time during the past winter, but he certainly seems to respect places where civilians are living. Also he may have wished to avoid any retaliations.

8.6.17
At 3 a.m. I roused MacDougall and lay down with my feet in water and with my steel helmet for a pillow. I slept for a few minutes only, when I opened my eyes and found MacDougall shaking me vigorously. 'Come on,' he said, 'get up. Fritz is coming.' 'I don't care,' I said, 'I'm tired', and turned over — but he pulled me up

and shouted that it was our relief that had turned up. So I staggered to my feet and got my equipment on. By this time Walker and all the other fellows except Aitken and myself were out of the dugout. I seized my lump of mouldy bread, picked up a tin of jam that belonged to somebody else, poured some of it on to the bread and shared it with Aitken. We were the last two in the file and I was feeling very fatigued when, stepping on a soft patch, I slipped and went over my knees into watery mud. Aitken helped me out but I was too exhausted to stand so sat down for about ten minutes to get my breath and a little strength. When we resumed, the remainder of the party were out of sight. We only had a vague idea of the direction in which we had to go, and after passing an immense mine crater (an old one) in the forward side of which Fritz had built some strong concrete dugouts, we eventually come to Stragglers Post. We had seen numerous dead bodies in all the ghastly horrors and mutilations of violent death, men with half their heads blown off and their brains falling over their faces — some with their abdomens torn open and their entrails hanging out — others stretched out with livid faces and blood-stained mouths, and unblinking eyes staring straight to heaven. Oh wives and mothers and sweethearts, what will this victory mean to you? Yet nature very readily adapts itself to its environment and can look on all these horrors without a shudder. But I should feel sick and almost terrified if I saw a man break his leg in the streets of London.

At Stragglers Post the guard could not direct

us to our Brigade HQ so we wandered here and there making scores of fruitless enquiries until suddenly we met Bill Rogers and his runners coming from the Relay Post. Of course they knew the way and took us only a short distance past Stragglers Post to the dugouts at ET10 (Voormezeele). This is the first deep dugout that I have been in since the Somme last October. It is about thirty feet deep and has two or three galleries. When we reported in at the Signal Office, Buchanan gave me a mug half full of rum but my hand was so shaky that I spilt most of it down my clothes. It was now 8.30 a.m. and for forty hours we had been on the go without food or sleep. Early in that period, too, my nerves had been badly shaken, so it is no wonder that I felt absolutely laid out. The cooks got us some breakfast and I almost fell asleep over it, and then lay down outside the entrance to the sap but was warned that it was not a safe place to go to sleep in as a man had been killed there yesterday. So I washed and shaved as well as my shaky hand would let me and went down the stairs. Sgt Oxley lent me his bed and an overcoat and I was soon fast asleep.

9.6.17
Slept most of yesterday and all last night so feel pretty fit today except that I am a bundle of nerves. Any sudden noise makes me give ridiculous involuntary starts so that I drop anything I happen to be holding. Watched some of our triplanes doing wonderful stunts such as

falling headlong for 300 or 400 feet as if they had been hit, and then righting themselves. Andy McCormack returned from leave. He was lucky in just missing this 'do'.

10.6.17

My hand still shakes too much to permit of letter writing without causing people to wonder what is the matter with me. This afternoon Davidson and I went up as far as the old no-man's-land and had a look at two of the new mine craters. One solid concrete dugout had been blown up and rolled over bodily. The dead body of a German was still inside. All our own dead have been buried but there are still a few German bodies scattered about. The RE Field Companies are working hard on pit-prop roads and trench tramways. They have carried them as far as the old front line and are now working across no-man's-land. Their hardest work is now commencing. It is an extraordinary scene of animation. Wagons and lorries full of materials are arriving in constant succession and hundreds of men are unloading and carrying and putting in place, all within easy reach of Fritz's artillery but he is not being very bothersome; probably he is tired after the big counterattack he made the night before last along the whole of the new front. He was repulsed everywhere although the attack lasted from 7 p.m. till midnight. The official reports issued to the English press state that all the objectives were captured early in the morning of the 7th, but we know that the 47th

Div. is still held up some distance from its final objective and it is quite likely that some of the Divisions on our right have failed to get as far as they were supposed to.

13.6.17

After breakfast I moved up with the Advance Party under Cpl Hamilton to Spoil Bank on the Ypres-Comines Canal. Our new quarters appear to be safe and quiet. Just at this spot the canal runs between two high banks or long mounds which look as if they may have been formed of the earth dug out to make the canal. Both banks are honeycombed with tunnels with additional detached dugouts here and there along their sides. Our office is known as ES09 and we are close to the old HQ of the Kents — ES29. A few yards in front of us is a lock which holds the water back so that only a little stream is leaking out and trickling along the bed. Here and there a shell hole has been utilised to collect the water for washing purposes. The saps are lit by electric light and are kept in repair by a permanent staff of Canadian Tunnellers. The general level of the floor of the galleries is practically the same as the towpath, so we have the advantage of twenty to thirty feet above us without the disadvantage of a long steep flight of steps. Four battalion signallers have joined us permanently which will make things a bit easier for us. The 47th Div. has had a very rough time and are glad to be relieved. It is rumoured that we are to take the objectives that they failed to reach. The casualties in our Brigade on the 7th were somewhere in the region of 300, which is light considering the nature of the operations. That, I presume, is why we have been selected to carry out this additional stunt. This evening Cpl Hamilton took a party up to our advance post at White Chateau. They are all men who stayed back at Voormezeele during the first attack.

14.6.17
Went on duty in the Signal Office at 5 p.m. It was my turn on the commutator (switchboard), a job that I have no particular liking for. I was kept busy by reason of the impending attack. At 7.30 p.m. the 11th RW Kents and the 18th KRRC [King's Royal Rifle Corps] operating with the 24th Division on the other bank of the canal made the attack, advanced about 1000 yards and consolidated the position before nightfall. Where the 47th Div. had failed, our troops succeeded easily; perhaps because Fritz was not expecting us. Buchanan was in the Signal Office all the time but said nothing to me, yet his presence is always sufficient to make me nervy. While the attack was in progress he sent for MacDougall to take over from me (MacD. is our best switchboard operator) and I was put on a 'Fullerphone'. This was more congenial work so I didn't greatly resent the imputation that I was lacking in efficiency on the commutator.

When I went off duty at 10 p.m., Buchanan followed me outside and stopped me in the passage. 'Martin,' he said, 'you mustn't take it

114

too much to heart that I put MacDougall in your place. You are apt to get a little flurried when I speak sharply but you mustn't think that I am cross — I am only anxious.' I thanked him and said that I knew I was naturally of a nervous disposition and that the shock I received on the night of the 6th-7th had made me much worse. 'I know,' he replied, as if somebody had told him all about it, 'and I quite understand so now don't worry any more and don't get upset when I shout and hustle.' He smiled when he wished me goodnight and I felt that I wanted to shake his hand for it seemed so wonderful to hear him talk so kindly after all these months during which I have thought he was 'up against' me. It seems a complete volte-face and I hardly know what to make of it. He has the reputation of not taking very kindly to strangers and perhaps he counts me a stranger no longer.

15.6.17

The Kents captured fifteen prisoners last night and six of them were killed by one of their own shells as they were being escorted back past White Chateau, which seems to be a veritable deathtrap as Fritz shells it unceasingly. We are so free from shelling here that several of our fellows have been bathing in the canal just above the lock, not a very wise thing to do as Fritz's balloons look right down on it. This afternoon, after a very heavy bombardment concentrated chiefly on the front line and the White Chateau, Fritz counter-attacked, but he was dealt with so efficiently by our artillery that only a few of his men reached our trenches where they were quickly repulsed. Cpl Hamilton has recommended Dickson for maintaining communications under very heavy shellfire between White Chateau and Brigade HQ.

18.6.17
On night duty last night and as things were fairly quiet I wrote half a dozen letters and now feel as if I had removed a load from my conscience. Transport can't get nearer to us than the Brick Stack so each evening we have to go down there and carry up our rations and supplies. How the army does live on rumours! The latest one is that we are to be relieved tomorrow, but I am beginning to mistrust the lying jade and never accept any of her promises until they are fulfilled.

19.6.17
Our relief turned up today and we moved back over a km of broken country to Elzenwalle Chateau. This was not a very big place as chateaux go and now it is only a mass of ruined masonry with only one small cellar inhabitable and that is used as our Signal Office. Although the country is torn to bits it is nothing like so bad as further up the line, and there are still a few cherry trees and currant bushes growing and bearing fruit, indicating the whereabouts of the

19.9.17

This morning I came up out of the tunnels and had a wash in a shell hole. Then I went to the top of the bank and had a look round. It was not safe so I didn't stay long. Looking towards the enemy (the front line is only 400 yards away) the land dips down into a slight valley, and on the hill beyond stands Gheluvelt which at this distance appears hardly to be touched. Tower Hamlets, our objective, is this side of Gheluvelt but on the other side of the valley. I counted a dozen derelict tanks and we call this neighbourhood 'Tank Cemetery'. Looking backwards over Zillebeke Lake, Ypres stands out grisly and white like a ghost of a city, and really that's all it is. This spot is certainly a vantage point. No wonder Fritz pays it so much attention. With the exception of short bits of trench at the entrances to the saps, the only shelter is to be found in shell holes. And half of each of these are filled with water. The Kents are lying back at Larch Wood. They were supposed to take over the tunnels there but when they arrived last night they found them crammed full of men of other units, so they had to remain in the open and have consequently suffered a good many casualties. The horses with the rations cannot get right up here so each night all men not on duty have to form a ration party and go and bring them up. After dark this evening we had to see the party off and help them a part of the way with their signalling equipment. It was pouring with rain and shells and I got wet through. Returning, I had got into the trench and was almost up to the door of the sap when a shell burst on the parapet and I was covered in mud and dirt, one piece giving me a whack on the top of the shoulder, but it was not sufficient to call for notice and I thought no more about it until later in the evening when something caused me to put my hand to the spot and I found a long scratch, no worse than a kitten would give. I am rather surprised because all I felt at the time was a thud as if a heavy clod of earth had struck me, but there must also have been a sharp little piece of something or other to go through my clothes and give me a scratch like this. Thank God it was no worse, though at times the strain of this existence makes one long for death.

20.9.17

I was awake when the attack started at 5.40 a.m. So I went up on top to watch it, but the barrage on both sides was so heavy that it was impossible to see any movement because of the smoke, but along the line of attack shells were bursting dozens at a time. It was safe enough now where I stood as the Hun was concentrating all his efforts on the line a few hundred yards in front of me, so I shaved and washed in a shell hole and about 8 o/c climbed to the top again to have another look at the attack. It was evident that things were not going so well as anticipated — the line had moved forward but it was still far from the final objective, and there was no doubt that Fritz was putting up a very fierce and stubborn resistance. The battalions making the attack were the Hants and the KRRs followed up by the Kents and the Surreys. On our left is the 23rd Division and on our right the 124th Brigade. I have been on duty in the Signal Office a good deal during the day and little bits of information have been trickling through regarding the progress of the attack. Putting them all together, the situation seems like this. Fritz had occupied some of the derelict tanks lying in no-man's-land and had made strongpoints of them. He fought desperately and disputed every inch of ground and his snipers remained at their posts, hidden in tree trunks etc, even after our troops had passed them, and continued to shoot our men from behind. One of them was captured badly wounded, and Col. Carey-Barnard, coming up, raised his revolver to kill him but seeing his terrible wounds refrained, and the wretch then pointed out where one of his sniping comrades was hidden. A machine-gun post in a pillbox held our men up for a long time. Our artillery played on it but could not get a direct hit. The Hants could get no further. They had lost all their officers and a great many men. Col. Corfe of the Kents tried to rally the men but was soon hit by a bullet in the shoulder, but he held on until the post had been outflanked. Then he collapsed.

20.9.17 cont.
It is now apparent that the attack has fallen considerably short of what was expected, but what can you expect from men who are tired and

hungry and wet through? To say nothing of the fierce opposition they have had to face. Our Advance Signals when they went up last night tried to establish themselves in a dugout but were peremptorily ejected by Col. Carey-Barnard who wanted it for himself. So they settled themselves in a little lean-to shelter behind the dugout. A stray dog that has somehow or other got up the line also tried to get in the dugout. He wouldn't stop in the shelter because it was only covered with corrugated iron and a few handfuls of dirt to camouflage it. During the morning Percy Mayne was wounded in the arm while bringing a message to Brigade HQ. He delivered it and then had to be carted off to the dressing station and so down the line. An American doctor who is attached to the Kents performed the operation of amputating a man's leg in the midst of the attack. I expect that tomorrow the English papers will be shouting the news of a great victory, but it has been a ghastly and murderous failure. A reinforcement arrived for us this evening — a young fellow just out from England. It's ridiculous to send a new recruit up to a place like this.

I was surprised to see some Military Police in these tunnels. They are the warriors who infest the rest areas and spend their time in 'running' poor unsuspecting Tommies who leave their cycles unattended for a few seconds. Their business up here is to prowl round the tunnels looking for men who have taken shelter when they ought to be outside. A miserably ignoble trade!

21.9.17

At 8.30 this morning the Sergeant sent for me. He directed me to take Cochran (the new man) and go to Sgt Jordan, who is in charge of the Signal Dump in Canada Tunnels, and bring back two drums of cable. It was wanted urgently as all our lines had been blown to smithereens and our supply of cable was exhausted. Immediately we got out of the sap I saw we were in for a rough journey as Fritz was giving us a most terrific shelling. Every conceivable type of shell was bursting all around, whizzbangs, HEs, HVs [High Velocity shells], liquid fire, gas shells and all manner of shrapnel, the latter bursting a dozen at a time. It was evident that Fritz was endeavouring to prevent any reinforcements coming up. When we got to the end of the little bit of trench I scrambled out, but Cochran lost his head and shouted out 'Don't go, don't go, we shall all be killed!' It was no time to be nice so I told him not to be a fool but to come along and I caught hold of him and pulled him up on to the parapet. A shell burst a little way away on our left and out of the smoke emerged two men, one supporting the other who had been badly hit. Another burst on our right and Cochran threw himself behind a pile of duckboards — I fetched him out and he hung on to my coat and tried to pull me into a shell hole. I coaxed him and cursed him but he hadn't a ha'porth of nerve and I literally had to drag him along. It was a thousand times worse than going by myself. When we got inside Canada Tunnels he recovered himself somewhat. I found Sgt Jordan,

153

an old soldier, and he refused to let me have the cable because I had not brought a demand note signed by an officer. He actually wanted me to go back and get it. I thought many strong things but I didn't say them — I talked nicely to him, pointed out the urgency and told him what a nice fellow he was. Eventually he agreed to let me have the two drums if I promised faithfully to bring back the demand note at once. I was in the mood to promise anything though I had not the slightest intention of keeping any promise I might make.

The drums weighed half a hundredweight each which is quite as much as any man would like to carry over this churned and muddy country. Before we left the tunnels I gave Cochran a good talking to and told him that we had got to get back to Hedge St. in the quickest possible time; therefore he had better not act the giddy ox but keep close behind me and only duck into shell holes if he saw me do it. I glanced back two or three times and saw that he was following although gradually the distance between us was increasing. After jumping over a fragment of trench I proceeded for about fifty yards before looking round and then Cochran was nowhere to be seen. I dumped the cable and was just going back to find him when he scrambled out of the trench, trembling and blubbering worse than ever. In his fright he failed to jump over the trench and dropped down right on to a dead body. It was some job to fetch him along after that but at last we got into the tunnels. The distance was only about 300 yards each way but it had taken two solid hours. While we were out Tom McLachlan and Alec Robertson were mending a line when a shell landed between them. McLachlan was killed outright and Robertson was wounded. In the afternoon the violence of the shelling had abated and I went out to have a wash. While I was dipping into a shell hole a piece of shrapnel hissed viciously past my ear into the water. I wonder how many scores of times sudden death has missed me only by inches, and yet other fellows get done in by almost the first shell that comes their way. One cannot help becoming fatalistic.

22.9.17
Last evening Fritz treated our front line to a hurricane bombardment and developed a counter-attack. Our men were quite exhausted and it is no wonder that some of them started to retire without receiving orders to do so. Col. Carey-Barnard and Major Pennell (KRR) drove them back at the point of the revolver. For some time the position was extremely critical but our artillery managed to stop the counter-attack. The troops are all mixed up, men of different units and even of different divisions are huddled together in the same shell holes. The Brigade Major has been up the line and has sent a secret report into Division. There is no doubting the seriousness of the situation for on the phone I overheard a most amazing conversation between our

Brigadier and the Divisional Commander. The Brigadier was very firm in his insistence that our Infantry is thoroughly exhausted and totally unable to make any resistance if the Huns attacked. They would break right through our line if once they got beyond our artillery barrage. The Div. Commander tried his hardest to get the Brigadier to say that we can hold on for another twenty-four hours but General Towsey wouldn't take the responsibility of making any such statement. Lawford, of course, is looking to the laurels of the Division and the honour that will fall to him. When Gen. Towsey told him that the men could get neither rations nor water he merely replied, 'Let them take the iron rations from the killed and wounded.' This conversation lasted about half an hour and I expect it will result in a speedy relief. This morning Dickson found McLachlan's body and took from it his pay book and personal property. The latter will be sent to his relatives in Blighty.

23.9.17
Late last night word came through that our relief was on its way up. We were to clear out before daylight but although we tried to get away about 3 a.m. we were subjected to various hindrances and dawn was breaking before we had got our stores loaded on to a trench tramway wagon. It was a slow procession as the tramway track was blown up every hundred yards or so and we had to lift the wagon loaded with stores across shell

holes. After about six of these adventures we met a very bad hole and decided to unload the wagon, carrying the things on our backs across the country till we should meet another truck. Fritz shelled us all the way but fortunately there were a large number of duds, the ground being so soft that the percussion was not sufficient to explode the shells. There were more stores than we could carry in one journey so we had to go back a second time. The distance was not far and just as we had put down the first load and were going back for the second a shell burst close to the wagon. A man who was making his solitary way down the line was very badly hit in the face and side and arm, his fingers were only hanging on by bits of skin. Two stretcher-bearers happened to be close by and they quickly carried him off. Just as we reached the wagon and were all crowded round it grabbing at the things in our haste to get back, another shell burst in the same place. The pieces flew all round us and over us and in between us but not one of us was scratched, whereas the other poor creature, making less than a twentieth of the target that we did, got so badly wounded. Such are the fortunes of war.

We lost no time in getting back and loading up on another truck. We were amongst the guns and we hurried to get beyond them because we knew that they were going to start a heavy strafe at 7.10 a.m. but we didn't quite manage it. Jackson was standing quite close to a 4.5 howitzer but didn't know it till it suddenly blazed forth and he jumped about three feet into the air. After wrestling the wagon over a few more shell holes we arrived at Jackson's Dump where we found the limber waiting for us. McCormack and Jamieson, who we had left behind to carry on the visual till 6.30, were also there. They had not been impeded with a wagon-load of stores and had taken a shorter route along the duckboards. We now began to breathe and our spirits rose for the going was easier and every step was taking us away from Hell. We got to Ridge Wood where we rested for a few hours and had some grub. When the cooks had cleared out from their cookhouse, one of them went back to look for a tin of milk only to find that the place was completely blown in. In the afternoon we were left to rest in a field for two or three hours. Lieut. Sylvester found a little shop, bought a lot of cigarettes and distributed them among us. We trained to Castre where we found the Transport had already arrived and had erected tents for us. Thoroughly worn out, it did not take us long to get to sleep albeit our only covering was our overcoats and Cochran didn't even have that as he had thrown it away in his fright in going up the line.

24.9.17
It was nice to wake up and find oneself breathing fresh air instead of the vile putrid solid stuff of the tunnels, to say nothing about the absence of shells and bullets. Apart from attending a clothing and equipment parade and taking an idle turn of duty in the Signal Tent we have been left to spend our time in resting and in getting

passably clean. Not having been able to write any letters for nine days, my first duty was to sit down and write to Mother and Elsie. Tomorrow I shall write some more.

26.9.17
The Staff Clerks tell me that we are going to the coast, to a place called La Panne. It sounds good but we can't tell what it will be like till we get there. 'The Crumps' (Divisional Concert Party) erected a stage and gave a performance this evening in the field in which we are billeted. It is now 9 p.m. and we have received orders to move tomorrow morning. We are going by bus.

27.9.17
Up very early, as usual when we are on the move; marched through the little town to a spot just beyond the railway station, where the whole Brigade embarked. It was two or three hours before we got under way but the day has been fine and we had a really enjoyable ride through Cassel and Berques (where we saw some 'Abdullahs', i.e. French North African Native Troops, who look very picturesque in their peculiar dress) and so to Leffrinckhoucke where we are stopping for one night only. It is only a small village and I have found nothing of particular interest in it. We are quartered in a barn and I have got hold of a wire-netting bed. Still feeling pretty weary, as soon as it got dark I retired to rest. Presently the anti-aircraft guns

got going and we heard the drone of an aeroplane overhead. The searchlights managed to pick it out and the other fellows called me to get up and see it, but it would take more than that to fetch me out of bed now. The journey tomorrow is to be continued on foot but the distance is not very great.

28.9.17
Today we can hardly believe our senses. Five days ago we were in the most horrible hell man ever created, and now — well, the difference is almost the difference between hell and heaven. We marched by a road running parallel with the coast to Adinkerke where we turned sharp to the left and so came to La Panne and the open sea. The morning was beautiful and sunny and the march was quite enjoyable. Along the road low sand dunes (and a canal) separated us from the sea; and little whitewashed cottages were dotted about here and there looking so bright and clean and cheerful, in such remarkable contrast to the filthy, dirty, gloomy condition of everything in the Ypres area. Arriving, we marched straight to our billet which is a hotel right on the seafront. Our wildest dreams had never pictured us coming to such a delightful spot as this. Of course there are no beds or easy chairs; not even lino on the floors, but pleasure and happiness is only comparative and this is bliss after our experiences of the last twelve months. We got here soon after noon. Aitken and Glasspoole had come on in advance and opened office. By 12.30

we had discovered a patisserie shop and Glasspoole and I stuffed ourselves with delicious French pastries and coffee. We don't mind this sort of warfare.

29.9.17
Strolled around the town this morning. It does not appear to have suffered any damage at all from shellfire or bombs and is fairly well populated with civilians. It is essentially a seaside resort but of course it has done nothing in that line since 1914 — consequently all the hotels and large boarding houses have been vacated by their tenants and are now occupied by troops. Our billet must have been quite a swanky place. The room I am in is in the front looking out to sea and has a small verandah where we can go and sit during the day. At night of course we have to obscure the windows thoroughly. The sands are most extensive, stretching north and south as far as one can see. When the tide is out it is almost a Sabbath day's journey to the water's edge. The ordinary seaside landladies and fleecing tradesmen have adjusted themselves to the changed condition of things and now cater for the simple wants of Tommy Atkins. McCormack, Dickson and I found a place this evening where we had eggs and chips and coffee. There are several such places about but most of them are perpetually crowded. This one, however, is in a back street, out of the usual run and therefore is not so heavily patronised.

30.9.17

Sat on the sands this morning and wrote some letters. The Crumps have started open-air performances on the beach. This evening they were selling rather elaborate souvenir programmes. Bought one to send to Elsie. Turned in about 9.30 p.m. and just before 10 o/c Veitch came in and started to congratulate me. I didn't know what it was about until he explained. I appear in orders, having been promoted Sapper from 1 June, which means that I've got a bit of back pay to pick up, and also that Buchanan must have put me forward when I was still believing myself to be under his frown. Roughly I shall draw about £3 back pay and that will be very acceptable in a place like this. The leave allotment has been considerably increased and I begin to feel that with a bit of luck my turn will soon come.

3.10.17

Have written lots of letters during the past three days as there is very little else to do. Am 'sweating' on leave very violently. At the rate the men are going, my turn cannot be far away.

4.10.17

Leave fever has reduced me to a frightful state of fidgets. Can't keep still for two minutes together. The public baths here have been taken over by the British troops and this morning I enjoyed the luxury of a real bath, with a Belgian soldier as my own particular attendant. We had to leave our clothes in an ante-room and I put my purse in my gas mask, but while I was soaking the Ypres dirt out of my skin, somebody pinched my purse. Fortunately there was not much in it, about 15/-, mostly English money which I had been collecting in anticipation of leave. My wallet with about 300 francs in notes I had left behind at the billet.

A few stray thoughts scribbled down at various times, often in moments of peril:

It is generally true that after passing through a period of suffering we remember the little bits of pleasure which attended it more than the suffering itself.

What are the frownings of Fortune compared with her favours?

Obscurity and happiness are enough for me.

Home is where the heart is.

Reunion — the bright star towards which we look with so much confidence.

Love belongs to the infinities, those things which in this life we can only vaguely grasp.

The language of the army is a psychological study. It is not a question of bad language as such — it is more the inadequacy of ordinary language to express feelings and emotions under great mental and physical strain, and when one is up against the harshest realities of existence, the strongest words seem pale and ineffectual. Love is love, but a fondness that is founded on superficialities may turn to hate.

The postbag is the oasis in the desert of our existence.

If you see that a question has two sides, and

decline to become violently partisan, people will call you weak — whereas you are really strong.

The best letters are never written on paper.

5.10.17
My leave warrant has arrived in the Brigade Office. It is dated for crossing on the 8th and according to the new regulations which came into force either today or tomorrow I ought not to have it until the 7th but Sgt Lunn says he will give it to me tomorrow morning if I call for it about 9 o/c. I shall not be late.

6.10.17
Up very betimes and packed everything up in readiness. Got away soon after 9 a.m. Tramped to the crossroads at the other end of the town and then jumped a lorry which took me very nearly to the gates of the Rest Camp where I reported to the Sergeant Major. He examined my warrant rather critically and said that he thought I should not have presented myself there until tomorrow. He was very hazy over the new regulations, so I begged him to let me go on today as I would prefer to spend the night in Boulogne. I certainly had no desire to stay at the Camp which was damp and dirty and inches deep in mud with only tents to sleep in and nowhere to go in the daytime. After some deliberation and conferring with one of his Sergeants he said, 'All right; fall in with today's party at 12.45.' I hung about watching the other

men come up and noticed that there were several others with passes dated for the 8th and the Sgt Major was getting windy about letting so many go through. At 12.45 we fell in and answered our names and then the SM called out, 'Fall out all those men with passes for the 8th'. About half a dozen fell out but I didn't move. He counted them and checked his list and said, 'There ought to be another'. After a few tense and anxious minutes during which he was hunting all over the place for my name, he gave up and ordered us to move on. I breathed more freely when we got out on the road. At Bray Station the passes were briefly scanned and stamped but I managed to crush through in a crowd and so on to the train where I chummed up with a motorcyclist corporal. We left Bray about 2.30 and crawled down to Calais which we reached between 8 and 9 and we marched across the town from one station to another. Here we had to wait for a couple of hours with only a small Salvation Army canteen anywhere near. It was a regular fight to get anything to eat but we managed it; and at 11 p.m. were crowded into trucks again and resumed our journey to Boulogne.

7.10.17
The night passed with the amount of discomfort usual to this method of travelling. We were crowded thirty or forty in a truck; it was impossible to lie down, the best we could manage was to sit on the floor with our knees up under our chins. Also we were unlucky in getting

an extra hour of it as Summer Time ended during the night. At daybreak we were still some distance from Boulogne but we arrived there about 8 o/c. The motorcyclist knew Boulogne and suddenly he said, 'Come on, let's jump out!' The train was going slowly across the points outside the station and by jumping out we avoided being taken a mile or two further on to a camp where they might have wanted to examine passes again, and in any case we should have had to march back to the docks. We walked along the metals through the station and out into the road. It was Sunday morning and not many people were stirring. We went over the bridge into the town and found a restaurant where we got some breakfast. Two MPs were on the bridge when we returned but did not stop us — their duty was to prevent men coming up into the town — and we were going out of it. Down on the quayside a notice instructed leave men to fall in at 11.30 so we just strolled about a bit and had a basin of porridge in Lady Angela Forbes' Canteen. The other troops were marched down and we fell in with them. Then commenced a close and careful scrutiny of our warrants by the MPs who came down the ranks. There was no evading it this time and I was ordered to fall out to the rear. About a dozen other men were in the same boat but as soon as the inspecting MP had got a little way down the line I fell in again and I expect the other fellows did the same. Then came another examination as we passed on the gangway and yet another when we stepped on to the boat. The first one was easy but at the latter we had to give up a portion of the warrant. With the help of the motorcyclist who crowded up behind me I handed my portion upside down and he thrust his own on top of it before the NCO could turn it over. We had only just got settled on the boat when the order came that we were to transfer to another boat as this one was not considered suitable for the very rough weather. There was no further examination of passes and at ¼ past 12 we started to move out of the harbour. It was a terribly rough voyage; our boat was blown right round three times. I was about the only one on board who was not seasick and we did not arrive in Folkestone until ¼ past 3. Trains were waiting and soon we were speeding up to London. As we looked out of the carriage windows it required a distinct effort to realise that the people we saw walking about were English and spoke the same language we did — so accustomed have we become to seeing only civilians of other nations who jabber in French or gargle in Flemish. Reached Victoria at 6 and Ealing Broadway before 7 p.m. To 76 Drayton Gardens where strangers admitted me, Mr and Mrs Berwick being at church. I washed, shaved and helped myself to a good meal and went down to the church and saw Mrs Berwick. On to 17 Hastings Road where I found Elsie alone — she had a feeling that I would come. Slept at no. 76 on a real bed with real sheets and a soft pillow. Thus did I arrive in Blighty a day before my time.

8.10.17–10.10.17
At Ealing seeing old friends.

11.10.17
To King's Lynn with Elsie to see Lil, Edward and Peggy.

13.10.17
From King's Lynn to Dunmow with Elsie. Was glad to see my mother again.

15.10.17
Returned to Ealing with Elsie. The time is passing quickly.

18.10.17
Up early and Elsie came to the Broadway with me. It was very hard to say 'Goodbye' but she was such a brave little girl and gave me such a bright smile as we parted. We detrained at Shorncliffe and marched into Folkestone where we were put into a quarter of the town near the harbour. The streets were barricaded and guarded so that we could not get out into the town. After several hours' dreary waiting we boarded the boat and reached Boulogne about half past four. From the harbour we were marched to St Martin's Camp on top of a hill. It is a hard pull up, especially after ten days of ease and comfort. We were immediately sorted out

into batches according to the different parts of the line to which we were going, and received instructions regarding our trains tomorrow. These camps are wretched places. I shall be glad to get back to my Brigade.

19.10.17
We were kept hanging about all the morning but eventually entrained. The journey was not such a long one as when we came down and we arrived at Bray at 11 p.m. Guides conducted us to the Rest Camp at Ghyvelde. Here we were put into a stable-like building with a floor partly of sand and partly of cement. Blankets were refused us; it was cold and cheerless and the stone floor was far from inviting. I took a piece of candle from my haversack, lit it and looked around. Several men were lying about trying to sleep. I chose a place next to a man who had covered his head with his overcoat. I threw my equipment off and growled. The overcoat moved, and who should look up at me but Davidson. He is going on leave. Lay down beside him for an hour or so but was much too cold to sleep — got up, stamped about to try and restore the circulation, then lay on the sand to see if that was any less cold than the cement, but it wasn't; on the other hand it seemed to be full of small objectionable creepy creatures so I got up and walked up and down till daylight.

20.10.17

As soon as it was light enough to see, Davidson and I had a wash and a shave in some water from which we had to remove the ice. After breakfast, nobody seeming to take any interest in us, and no orders having been issued as to what we were to do, I decided to make my own way up to Brigade. Davidson told me they had moved from La Panne to Coxyde Bains and directed me how to get there so I jumped a lorry which took me some distance and then I walked the rest. After Boulogne and Ghyvelde it's a relief to get back to Brigade. I was just in time for dinner — the new cook is a decided improvement on Gould, but new brooms sweep clean — time will prove his real worth. I have had a look round and made myself acquainted with the run of the place and now (7 p.m.) I feel tired out and am going to turn in. Lieut. Sylvester left Brigade and went back to Division a few days after I went on leave. From what I can make out Twycross worked it, but he only stepped out of the frying pan into the fire for now we have got Lieut. Purvis as our officer — commonly known as 'Jessie' because of his somewhat peculiar mannerisms.

22.10.17

Went to The Crumps this evening. They are going to England in a few days and there is some talk of their appearing at one of the London theatres or music halls. A most cheerless day, with leaden skies and plenty of rain but no mud! The sandy tracks have their advantages.

23.10.17
Coxyde Bains was evidently a rather select watering place of modern growth. There is an old port close to the beach, consisting of tall, gaunt, unhandsome fishermen's dwellings but the greater portion of the village is covered with the type of house known as 'arty'. The whole place is built on sand and there are only two made roads running through the village, the rest are only sand tracks. The Signal Office and Brigade HQ are in the nucleus of the village where the houses are clustered a little closer than elsewhere; the Transport Lines are near the beach, while our billet is in a pair of semi-detached villas at one end of the village, and is connected to the Signal Office (about 300 yards away) by one of the sandy roads which makes the journey seem four times its length. We also have telephonic communications between the Office and the billet. This has advantages but it also has drawbacks. The village has suffered a certain amount, from shell fire, particularly in the vicinity of the Signal Office, but the majority of the houses have not been irreparably damaged and still contain articles of furniture which were left by their owners when they fled hurriedly earlier in the war. It is a criminal offence to move any piece of furniture even from one house to another.

When the Brigade moved in here, about two

days before I got back, the Signals were given a billet close to the Office. The runners had a house which contained real beds and they congratulated themselves. But during the second night there was a little shelling and one seemed to give the house rather a shaking but Fisher, Southwood and Co. were comfortably in bed and wouldn't get up for anything. In the morning they found the dining room out in the middle of the road. A small shell had come through the window, burst in the room and blown the wall out. The Brigadier ordered a move and so we got our present billet which, being the last house in the village, is as safe as anywhere could be, as Fritz gives his attentions only to the main road, the 'nucleus' and the Transport Lines. He does a ten-minute strafe every evening at dusk and sometimes also at 10 p.m. Such regularity is commendable — we know what to do — but occasionally he breaks forth at a different time and so catches us on the hop. I share a small room on the first floor with Hamilton and Rogers. Our room contains a table, a bureau, an overmantle and a couple of chairs. A French window opens on to a little verandah from which we can safely watch the shells dropping on the beach or in the village. Two or three civilians (including one woman) still remain in the place but they are looked on with suspicion as the whole neighbourhood is chock full of spies. I understand the 123rd Brigade caught seven in the fortnight they were stationed here. Every night we can see rockets go up from the German lines at Nieuport and

172

answering rockets ascend from lonely spots on the dunes and marshes behind us. The country by its nature lends itself to this method of espionage. It is all marshland or rough sand dunes and a person knowing the land would stand a good chance of evading any pursuers.

26.10.17
Wrote to Mother telling her that I am trying to get Separation Allowance for her. She is distressed over my wangling an extra day's leave, is afraid I shall get into trouble! Played the piano in the NCOs' Mess this evening.

28.10.17
A day of great excitement. Our move forward has been cancelled, all men on leave have been recalled and we have had to pack up in readiness for moving off at a moment's notice. Rumour is very busy, but the only thing that is definite is the secrecy regarding our ultimate destination. Played the piano for nonconformist services this morning and again this evening.

29.10.17
Roused early this morning with orders to pack the wagons at once. Things very lively with all the bustle attendant on a hurried move. Transport got away early. The 15th Division is relieving us. MacDougall met one of their advance party who asked him what Division we

were. 'Forty-first,' said Mac. 'Lord,' replied the other, 'the blood and lust division!' So now we know what our nickname is among the rest of the army. It appears that we have the reputation for making things so unpleasant for Fritz that he retaliates strongly, and other divisions do not like following us in the line. General Towsey is on leave. The Acting Brigadier is Colonel Pennell of the 18th KRRC who at the beginning of the war was a corporal in the Regular Army. Sgt Twycross and I were left to close the Office and early in the afternoon walked about a mile to a spot where a motor lorry was waiting for us. We arrived at St Pol adjoining Dunkirk about 5 p.m. having caught up the rest of the Brigade HQ. Cpl Erith had been looking round for billets which he said were very hard to obtain, so we didn't expect anything great but what we got is even worse than we foreboded.

Situated in the main street running from Dunkirk along the coast towards Calais, trams pass the door every quarter of an hour. Houses and shops on each side of the road are closely built and yards are entered by large double doors always kept closed, a smaller one being cut in them to allow of individual passage. Such is the entrance to our billet and it will be difficult to find in the dark. Inside the doorway the upper storey of the house extends and forms an archway as in the old posting houses in England. Beyond is a pebble-paved courtyard with the entrance to the house on the right, next door wall on the left and our billet at the far end. A chicken run occupies one corner of the yard but cannot be described as ornamental. The inside of our billet, however, is the great feature. It is a cowshed with a gangway down the middle and ox stalls on either side. Certainly it has been swept out since the last cow died but chickens have had free access — we drove half a dozen out when we came in. There is a loft approached by a shaky ladder and the roof is far from watertight. I managed to settle in one of the least draughty corners on the ground floor and then Dickson and I went out to look for grub. After a little searching we found an estaminet up a side street where apparently they serve dinners every evening. This is fortunate.

30.10.17
Rumours have been many and varied as to why we have been taken from the line so abruptly. At first we were rather inclined to think it meant Ypres again, as we seem fated to spend much of our time in that area, but I don't think we should have been brought here if we were going back to the old sector. Egypt, Italy and Ireland are all strong favourites in the Rumour Race, but I think Ireland can be struck out and, as regards the other two, I am rather inclined to think it will be Italy, in view of the big reverses the Italians have had lately. On the other hand, we only know what is published in the papers and it is quite possible that trouble has arisen in Ireland or Egypt or

sell us bootlaces but the crowd pounced on him and dragged him out of our way. There was much gesticulating and shouting but we turned a corner so could not see what transpired.

The Brigadier stood on the steps of a hotel and took the salute as we marched past. Crowds of children ran along beside us for miles. We marched cheerfully although we soon felt the effects of five days lazing in the train, and eventually arrived at Guidizzolo. In the town we were not quite certain of our way and called to some Italian soldiers. They didn't attempt to understand us but set up a hue and cry, which resulted in the finding of a soldier who could speak English, or rather American. Our billet is a respectable loft and the Signal Office is in the centre of the town. Rumour says that we have five days' marching in front of us. This evening Dickson and I had sausages and potatoes in a Trattoria just outside the billet. Don't know what the sausages were made of and perhaps it is as well not to enquire. Distance marched today = 17½ miles.

18.11.17
Thousands of retreating Italians passed through here this morning. They looked a pretty rabble. Had thrown away all their equipment; the only things they retained other than what they stood up in were their overcoats and these were loaded in piles on little mule-or donkey-carts, strange looking vehicles to our idea of transport. The men were straggling along rather than marching,

albeit their pace was rather fast. There was very little order, they only seemed intent on getting away from the line as quickly as possible. In the afternoon Jessie S. held an inspection of all Signal Stores and our own personal equipment. He gave us a lecture on the arduous nature of the march in front of us and said that nothing was to be taken unless absolutely necessary; therefore he condemned the football to be dumped but I bet it turns up when we want it. A quantity of signal stores was packed into hampers and sealed down; these are to be left here until we can send back for them. The Post Office men are billeted in a Trattoria near the Signal Office and this evening Dickson and I joined them in a supper of stewed hare and polenta. We enjoyed it. The polenta stuff seems quite harmless and is filling. English rations have not arrived so we have been issued with Italian. Wrote several letters but Corporal Smith says he doesn't know when they will go away.

19.11.17
Roused early to get cleaned up so that we may make the necessary impression on the civilians. Jessie made me take the piece of rag off the muzzle of my rifle as it was very unsightly. Put it in my pocket and replaced it at the first halt. It may not be ornamental but it keeps the damp and dirt out of the barrel and is therefore a labour-saving device, reducing the amount of cleaning to a minimum. At midday we had an hour's halt and discovered a remarkable

difference between the temperatures in the sun and in the shade. We were very hot with marching, and immediately sought the shelter of some trees but it was surprisingly cold, dangerously so in fact; so we emerged into the sunshine again and nibbled our biscuits and bully by the side of the clear little stream running merrily by the roadside. We were very tired when we arrived at Mozzecane where a lot of Italian soldiers were billeted in a place that may be a barracks. Our home for the night is a farm at the north end of the town. We were marched into the yard and left standing for several minutes when the Brigade Major came up and told Mr Jamblin to order us to remove our equipment and to fall out, it being necessary in view of possible heavy taxes on our energies in the near future, that we should be given every possible opportunity to rest. Distance marched today = 17 miles. Total = 34½ [miles].

20.11.17
Last night I was on night duty with Enticknap. The Signal Office was in a stone-floored room which was part of the farmhouse and was half filled with a heap of wheat. On this we each managed to get about two hours' sleep but we had to start rousing the troops at 4.30 a.m. Today's march was very trying.

It happened today that one of our ten-minute halts occurred in a small hamlet. Of course the inhabitants crowded out to see us and one of them suddenly had a brainwave. There was a little jabbering and then a rush indoors and in a few seconds the women returned with, not just glasses or mugs, but buckets of red wine; and when they were emptied they went back and were refilled. Jessie got the wind up. He was afraid we should all get 'cut', but a few buckets don't go far amongst a crowd of thirsty men. We were feeling whacked when we arrived at Isola della Scala, an unpretentious little town with no features of outstanding interest. We knew this to be our resting place for tonight and as we marched through the streets we kept our eyes open for restaurants. As soon as we were settled, Hamilton and I made our way into the town, found a Trattoria and had a feed of macaroni and horseflesh. It was a strange dish but we were starving and had to fill ourselves up with something or other.

For a long while this afternoon, General Lawford and General Towsey were earnestly engaged in conversation in the road outside our billet. On Brigade HQ we have been grousing heartily about marching on short rations but the men in the battalions have been shouting a bit louder and things had arrived at the point when Regimental Commanders begin to wonder whether their authority will be recognised for many more hours. The Surreys, who had to proceed a few kms beyond this town, halted here for an hour to have their midday meal consisting of bully and biscuits. Breakfast had consisted of similar articles and they had marched ten or twelve miles. While they were halted, who should come along but the Prince of Wales. The men recognised him and greeted him by holding up the bully and biscuits and shouting, 'How'd you like to do twelve miles on this with a full pack?' Of course those Staff Officers who are doing the journey in motor cars and having three or four good meals a day are quite ready to move on, but it looks as if there will be trouble if we don't soon get a little rest or some substantial meals or both.

Rumours kept flying about that we are to have a day's rest but the official order did not arrive until 9.30 p.m. We raised a cheer of thankfulness for I don't think any of us feel fit for another march tomorrow. Incidentally, I think it has averted the possibility of trouble in the battalions. Men can be driven and bullied a long way under a military system that continually holds out the 'FP No. 1' and 'Shot at dawn' threats, but there is a limit to human endurance of despotic government, and we have nearly reached it. Distance marched today = 13 miles. Total = 47½ [miles].

21.11.17
Walked in the town and bought some picture postcards. By the way, we are now allowed to tell our people at home that we are in Italy, but for my part I had already sent word by Tom Glasspoole when he went back on leave just before we left Dunkirk. Even the most severely enforced restrictions can be surmounted or undermined where one has the will to do it — just like Acts of Parliament — none has yet

been framed but that a coach and four horses could be driven through it. Went inside the church and had a good look round; it is ornamental in a costly and rather gaudy fashion. The local bakers have been working continuously ever since we arrived yesterday but they cannot cope with the demand. British soldiers are lined up in hundreds outside every baker's shop waiting for the next batch of bread to come from the ovens. The cafés have all been crowded out all day long — they can never have done such a trade in the whole of their existence.

22.11.17

The day's rest has done us good and has soothed the spirit of unrest so we did not grumble much at having to get on the move again early, this morning. We marched well and at midday crossed over the huge iron bridge spanning the Adige into Albaredo. On the move every day, it is not an easy matter to keep in touch with all the units and we all have to take turns assisting the DRs [Despatch Riders] to find them. Our directions are generally vague and the maps we have are far from reliable. So it happened this afternoon that I was sent with a message to the Field Ambulance. The only direction I received was that the FA had been seen to turn to the left at the end of the street. I soon came to another T-road and took the most likely looking turning to the right. Crossing a stream, the road divided and I didn't know which fork to take. A Corporal of the RAMC came up and I thought I was lucky. He said, 'Oh it's up this way.' So away we rode together, turned into a side road and struck the 124th Brigade HQ. He had to admit he had taken the wrong road so we set off again and eventually arrived back in Albaredo after a circuit of ten miles or more. It was quite a pleasant ride in beautiful weather and interesting country. Passing through the town, we crossed the little bridge again and took the other turning and soon came to the Ambulance billeted in a farm. After dark I had to go out there again and on the return journey bore to the side of the road to avoid a heavily laden farm wagon and ran up on to a great heap of stones and came a cropper. Grazed my hand and bruised my shin a little.

Taylor was trying to find his way this afternoon when he came to a road fork that was not indicated on the map. He accosted an Italian soldier — held his map out, performed a variety of extraordinary deaf and dumb show (he had given up trying to make himself understood by talking) and after a few minutes the Italian said in English, 'Well now, what the blankety blank do you want?' Distance marched today = 15½ miles. Total = 63 [miles].

23.11.17
Resumed our march in good spirits although some of the fellows complain of blisters on their feet. I take as much care of mine as possible, wearing only the socks that Elsie knitted for me. As soon as a hole develops I put on another pair

and pack the old ones away for washing and darning at the first opportunity. The inaccuracies of the Italian maps led us to trudge two or three miles further than we need to have done. We turned along a good road which seemed to be the correct one but after nearly a mile it gradually deteriorated into a lane and finished up by landing us in a field. We just had to turn round and work our way back again. We have travelled in a north-easterly direction today and the mountains have become appreciably nearer. We halted for ten minutes in Lonigo which is Corps HQ. It is the largest town we have entered so far and was merrily decorated with flags and bunting and huge notices placarded on the walls greeting us with:

Good Health at the Allies
Bravo L'esercito Inglesi
Good Health at the England
Welcome at the Allies and co

Lonigo lies at the foot of the Monte Berico, a small spur of the Alps. A reasonably level road cuts through them to Vicenza but our route tomorrow is to be over the top. After leaving Lonigo we began to climb — a good road and not very steep but a decided change after the extreme flatness of the country which we have traversed up to the present. Passed through the little village of Sarego to a chateau standing on the hillside. Arriving at the entrance to the carriage drive we halted to get a little breath and energy to enable us to climb to the chateau which was almost straight above us. As we rested, the Surreys passed us toiling up the hill to the next village. The Brigadier was standing with us and of course the Surreys' Officer Commanding started to call his men to attention but the Brigadier waved his hand and said, 'No, no, let the men march easy.' Some of them seemed to be getting done up and I noticed one officer carrying four men's rifles. Our final ascent to our billet was by a winding drive between trees and tall shrubs. It was short but it was severe and it made us puff and perspire. Fortunately Lally managed to get his mules up with the stores so we were saved the trouble of carting them up. Our billet is a granary containing plenty of straw. A lot of chickens were running about; they belonged to an adjacent cottage, probably the gardener's home, so I went up there and tried to get some eggs. Although I used my finest Italian accent in pronouncing the word 'uova' it was quite impossible to make the old lady understand. She tried me with a chair, then a table, and finally offered me her whole sitting room. I gave it up and returned to find that her husband had taken a basket full of eggs and was selling them to the men at the billet. Jessie took MacDonald's motorcycle and went off to prospect the road we have to travel tomorrow. He came back with a tale of frightful mountains, narrow roads and steep precipices. We know he is given to exaggeration; still, there is no doubt that we are in for a very stiff time. Distance marched today = 15 miles. Total = 78 miles.

24.11.17

Reveille at 4 a.m. Packed the limber. Breakfast at 5.30 consisting of a plate of porridge and biscuit and cheese. The heavy transport left at 3 a.m. taking the longer but more level road — only the light limbers accompanied us. We had to carry full packs including overcoats. I sorted out all the heaviest articles, including half my ammunition, and packed them in my blankets, but even then I suppose I was carrying about 80lbs on my back. We moved off at 6.45 a.m. and the going was fairly easy for the first few miles until we reached Brendola. Here we turned to the left and began the serious ascent, and a party was told off with ropes to help pull up the limbers. It is on hills like these that mules prove themselves superior to horses. They will pull and pull whereas horses soon lose heart and give up trying to do a job which really they have plenty of strength to accomplish. Only a few yards up the hill we passed a Surrey limber stuck by the roadside. The horse, a great strong animal, merely looked at the hill, sighed, and refused to budge even though all the weight of the load was being taken by a platoon of men pulling on the ropes. The road twisted and turned and took us up nearly 1000 feet, the summit of the hills being 400 or 500 feet higher. The hills, being of volcanic origin, are extremely irregular and consequently the road was a continuous series of twists and bends and wriggles. The morning was cold and the hills were wrapped in mist, white and damp and chilly. Sometimes we could see only a few yards on either side. In places the road ran along the edges of precipices and there was none too much room for the transport wagons; in fact it was a very ticklish job to get past some of the great lumbering oxen carts that we met. At midday we halted for an hour, having reached the highest point of the road. Our only food was the iron rations we carried — bully and biscuits again. Now we were glad of our overcoats for the mist kept sweeping down from the summits and making us shiver. Gradually and in spasms it lifted, giving us a glorious view over the country to Vicenza. We could see the long white road and the railway running side by side in the valley and in the distance rose the mountains of the Trentino, whilst nearer, nestling in the dark background of spreading vineyards, were numerous little white-housed villages with their quaint church towers. The view was worth the climb. When we got on the move again the sun had dispersed the mist and beat down on us pitilessly. The road was up and down and in and out until we came to the final descent to the plain which was by a series of four hairpin bends made necessary by the fact that the gradient of the hillside was about 1 in 1½. Now the men with the ropes had to act as brakes, for it was more than the horses and mules could do to hold the limbers back. It is reported that one or two went over but I do not know if this is true. All of ours completed the journey safely. As we reached the bottom, Divisional HQ were passing along. They had travelled by the level road that skirts the hills on the south and east. We turned to the left and sighed with relief as we looked along the level road in front of us leading to Longara and straightened our aching backs in a final endeavour to show the natives that twenty miles with a heavy pack was a mere bagatelle. But we were in for a most cruel disappointment. Captain Reiner and Sgt Lunn, who had come on in advance, met us and told us that our destination had been altered. We had to go several kms further on. This was the last straw, but we had to carry it. So with 'Stick it, boys' we strode breast forward but it was hard work. There was no energy for singing or whistling now; gradually we got out of step, and just as the shutters of heaven were being put up we stumbled into the little village of Costozza. A voice called out, 'Keep going, it's only another hundred yards' but my eyes were getting misty, the road moved up and down trying to evade my dragging feet — MacDougall, who was next to me, shouted, 'Stick it, Joe, the Signals never fall out!' It required a big effort to keep myself from falling but I kept up until we halted in the grounds of an enormous chateau. Then we lay down full length for a few minutes until we had recovered sufficient strength to climb to our billet in some of the rooms at the top of the building. Our entrance is at the back and we ascend by a wide staircase that would do credit to a public building in London. This is just the servants' quarters; what the remainder of the house is like passes imagination.

Once our oppressive equipment was removed we began to recover and our thoughts turned to food. The cooks couldn't get anything ready for an hour and we were empty. We had marched twenty-two miles, heavily equipped, over a range of hills that would be looked on as mountains in England and our rations for the last twenty-four hours had consisted of one small plate of porridge, a piece of cheese, a third of a tin of bully and a few bits of biscuit. So with shaking knees and our belts pulled tight, Hamilton, Aitken, Rogers and I went into the village to look for grub. We went all over it but couldn't get even a piece of bread. We had nearly given up in despair when we noticed a door beneath an archway. Through the crack shone a light, so we opened it and walked into a large room containing several tables, a counter and an enormous fireplace. The latter was situated on a raised platform at one end of the room and was by far the biggest fireplace I have ever seen. On the platform immediately in front of the huge fire were two or three small tables at which were sitting the ancient worthies of the village sipping vino buono and talking, probably about us. Women were serving wine and preparing a meal but it was several minutes before anybody took any notice of us.

Then an Italian officer who was sitting at one of the tables by the fire came and spoke to us in French. We told him that we wanted food and drink and didn't care what it was or how much it cost. He spoke to one of the women who then came over to us and by various gesticulations and a few stock words we managed to convey to her that we were starving. She nodded, looked affable, went away, and appeared to forget us. We discussed whether we should stop. Things did not look very promising. Probably our hunger made the time seem longer than it was. Food was being dished up and taken into another room but none came our way. A huge cake of polenta, steaming hot and covered with a thin white cloth, was brought from somewhere or other and placed on the counter. We decided to have a lump of that even if we had to take it but just as we were beginning to feel really desperate the woman came and laid a cloth for us. Then followed a bottle of wine and presently she brought plates and knives and forks. Our spirits rose but gradually descended as nothing further appeared. Hungry men are apt to be impatient. But there was some mysterious cooking going on at a little fire in a corner, and presently, to the joy of our hearts, came along some warmed-up chicken and several chunks of polenta. Did we enjoy it? Well, I think this will stand out as one of the very finest meals that I have ever had. Apart from the fact that it was food and that we were hungry, it will be memorable for it was so extraordinary to find something other than polenta and coarse sausages.

Distance marched today = 22 miles. Total = 100 miles.

25.11.17
It was no easy task to get up when we were roused at 5 a.m. Another long march was in front of us but fortunately without hills. It was still dark when we had our breakfast of porridge

and biscuits and bully. We ought to have had bacon but during the night some thieving Italians had stolen it. They had cut all the meat off and left us the bones. We presume the thieves were some Italian soldiers who were hanging round when we arrived last night. Eight o'clock saw us on the road again but we were not carrying our overcoats. Naturally we felt the fatigue of yesterday — but it is remarkable how a few hours' rest will restore one's energies. Nevertheless we began to tire early in the day, the kms were long and the hourly halts seemed far apart and to add to our troubles most of us were suffering from diarrhoea. But we kept our spirits up, singing and talking and reminding each other that while we were marching we were not fighting; and this thought is certainly a consolation particularly in a strange land with an enemy we know nothing about except that he has chased our Allies in one of the biggest drives of the war. The number of little cemeteries that we have passed today has been noticeable. They are really the equivalent of our churchyards but they never adjoin the church. Usually they are some little distance from the village and are all of the same pattern, rectangular in shape and enclosed by a high wall. Cypress trees, generally four, stand at the gateway, mute sentinels to keep the ghosts from straying. Iron crucifixes of varying size and ornamentation take the place of our headstones, ranging from small ones about eighteen inches high to tall ones that overtopped the wall.

Distance marched today = 17 ½ miles. Total = 117 ½ [miles].

26.11.17

The Signal Office is in a small cellar adjoining our billet and as there was nothing to do except to keep awake, Enticknap and I divided the duty, each spending the other half in his blankets. I worked the shift from 10 p.m. to 3 a.m. and spent the time in writing to Elsie. Sent the letter in a green envelope accompanied by the piece of maidenhair fern I plucked at Nice. We have got hold of some English papers; they are a fortnight old, but we have heard that there has been a British advance at St Quentin. No details have come to hand but of course we hope it is something good. At 3 a.m. 'Enty' relieved me and I curled myself up and slept like a log. Breakfast was delayed until 9 o/c in order to give us a little extra rest but no one was ready to get up even then. Dickson fetched my breakfast for me, as, having been on night duty, I was privileged to remain in 'Kip' as long as I liked. Later I rose, tended my blistered feet, and went out to survey the neighbourhood. Campo San Mattino is a tiny village hanging on the skirts of a great mansion which is the summer home of Count Breda, the Italian Railway Engineer. It is a wonderful building but we are allowed only in the commodious cellars. The grounds are large with big glass houses running up one side encasing lemon trees bearing ripening fruit. The fronts of these houses are all doors which are opened during the daytime and closed at night. There is ample first-class stabling and plenty of accommodation for coachmen and their families. Some of the trusted vassals are still in residence but of course Mr and Mrs Breda are many miles away.

In one of the cellars are several tons of coal, a very unusual sight in this country; and in the largest cellar, where most of the men are sleeping, is a huge boiler for supplying hot water to the baths. The Staff Officers wanted to indulge this morning so Sgt Oxley tackled the boiler with the result that the billet got half flooded before he had satisfied himself as to how it worked.

28.11.17
Left Campo San Martino after an early breakfast. The rest has done us good but hasn't healed our blistered feet. In passing through Campo Sampiero (which looks a quaint and interesting place) we met with a reception less frigid than we have hitherto experienced. In the town, market day was in full swing and some of the walls were covered with huge placards inscribed similarly to those we saw at Lonigo. Bunting and flags of various nations fluttered from the windows and across the narrow streets while the marketing populace stood and gazed and gabbled with amazement, occasionally raising their hats and bowing to us. Innumerable turkeys, geese and ducks were being bought and sold, all of them tied by a string round their legs, with a small child at the other end of the string dragging the poor birds hither and thither. Many of the birds are brought into the market tied by the legs in a bundle, and hanging head

downwards over the handlebars of 'comic' bicycles. They look more resigned than happy. A small pig with the ubiquitous string round its leg escaped from its owner, got in amongst our legs and caused great amusement. Immediately a crowd of excited natives started a chase and the pig gave them a good run for their money; in fact the chase was still in progress when we passed out of the town. I wish we had halted there for the night — it would have been more enjoyable than this dreary little village (St Andrea). Passed a street organ standing derelict in a field. This is the first we have seen as their public use is forbidden for the duration.

Distance marched today = 16½ miles. Total = 134 [miles].

29.11.17
Today's journey being reasonably short, we were not roused inordinately early but were on the move before 9 a.m., heading straight for the line. Passed the aerodrome at Fossalunga where the first contingent of our Air Force has just arrived. About noon we saw the first sign of actual warfare — an Italian heavy gun mounted in a meadow on the plain and firing over the hills. Every time it fired, the native women dashed about in a frenzy, shrieking and waving their arms as if they had gone mad. Soon afterwards the road gradually deteriorated until it was only a cart track across fields and it seemed that we had gone astray. So when we came to a point where the track branched off in two different

directions, Lieut. Tamblin halted us and sent the MMPs [Mounted Military Police] forward to reconnoitre with the result that we ultimately reached Musano early in the afternoon without having gone very far out of our way. The closest study of these execrable maps will not reveal the actual route we have traversed. We are billeted in the hospital with a few Italian soldiers. One of them has been teaching MacKay to count up to twenty in Italian. Managed to get three eggs which I boiled hard and ate in the hope that they will put a stop to this abominable diarrhoea. There seems to be a shortage of drinking water in this village, a state of things which we have not encountered anywhere else in this country. There is plenty of wine but it is almost impossible to get a bottle of water. I tried several of the peasants and at last found one who had a large glass wine jar full of water. He filled my bottle so I am all right for tomorrow. There is a large wooden crucifix about ten feet high and on it are carved all the emblems and tokens of the Crucifixion from the cock that startled St Peter to the spears and the sponge of vinegar. I am glad the journey has been fairly short today for I have felt far from well and could not take much interest in the incidents of the march.

Distance marched today = 8 miles. Total = 142 [miles].

30.11.17
Aitken, Mennie and MacDougall went forward by lorry this morning as an advance party to

commence taking over from the First Division of the Italian army in the line. We followed later in the day, our start being delayed so that the final stages should be taken under cover of darkness owing to the superiority of the enemy aircraft. The mountains seem to be getting mighty close although actually they are some twenty miles away. The march was slow as the roads were very narrow and congested with traffic. In passing some of our big motor lorries, the limber went into the ditch. The mules steadfastly refused to pull it out. Cajolings, threatening, thrashings, all were of no avail so we unharnessed them and half a dozen of us pulled the limber out easily despite being hampered by our equipment. And these are the same mules that pulled over the Monti Berico like Trojans! We were halted in one of the narrow roads when darkness overtook us and we were forbidden to smoke or strike matches. At a crossroads nearby, our valiant APM [Assistant Provost Marshal], cavorting on his charger, was going blue, black and purple with the violence of his efforts to direct the traffic. Soon it became evident that the road we were in was impassable for transport so I was told off to accompany the wagons by another route. Turning round in a field, we journeyed back and finally linked up with Brigade HQ in Selva. Our billet is in some farm buildings on the outskirts of the village but the moonlight is not sufficient for us to see much.

Distance marched today = 6 miles. Total = 148 [miles].

1.12.17

The night passed off quietly and although we are supposed to be quite close to the line we heard no sound of gunfire. Each of us managed to get about four hours' sleep, and after breakfast, as further slumber was out of the question, we made a tour of inspection of the village and neighbourhood. On the north, the Montello Hills rise very abruptly from the plain. A road and a small river run side by side along the base of the hills and directly you leave the road and cross the river you start a hard climb. These hills form a rather curious geographical feature. In some measure foothills to the main Alps, they are nevertheless an isolated kidney-shaped bump rising 368 metres (about 1200 feet), with the formidable Piave bounding them on the north and east. From a military point of view they are of great importance, commanding the whole of the level ground for many miles to the south. The stream that runs round this side of the hills is an offshoot from the Piave, breaking away from the main river at a point north-west of the hills and rejoining it on the south-east. Thus the whole range is virtually an island, and is crossed by twenty roads running north and south and known by numbers, no. I being the most easterly and no. 20 the most westerly. Along the top of the range runs a connecting road from east to west. The village itself is a dreary looking place crowded out with refugees from the east of the Piave, and there is nothing to buy, not even polenta. After an early tea we started off on the final stretch of our historic march. The distance was about two miles, but what miles! In addition to our ordinary equipment we had to carry overcoats and blankets. The roads were rough and steep and by no means gradual. Frequently we dipped down into little valleys or basins, only to have a stiffer climb out of them. After going for half an hour we had to fall out for fifteen minutes' rest. The Italians, I believe, only march fifteen minutes at a stretch in this sort of country. We eventually reached the summit of Road 8 and found Aitken and Co. waiting for us at a little deserted cottage. I was very tired, so, thanking God that all the marching is over for a bit, I quickly rolled myself up in my blankets and went to sleep.

Distance marched today = 2 miles. Total = 150 [miles].

2.12.17
It is hard to believe that we are really in the line for all last night we were not disturbed by a single shell, and in looking round about the billet in all directions it is difficult to discover any signs of war, that is, the sort of signs we have been used to. I feel very weak and tired and hungry. What wouldn't I give for a piece of bread in place of these eternal biscuits that I have to crush into powder with my pliers before I can eat them. I take the jam (when we get any), chop the margarine into small pieces and mix the lot up together and eat with a spoon. It takes about half an hour to crush up sufficient biscuit for one meal.

3.12.17

An Italian Labour Company is working in our vicinity making trenches and barbed wire entanglements, and they are making them well. It is amusing to see how they scuttle for shelter at the slightest alarm. We cannot help laughing as, compared with Ypres and the Somme, this is like being back at rest.

4.12.17

A visual post has been established a few hundred yards away and all of us who were not on duty have been over there to build a sandbag hut for the operators. Killed a snake about two feet long. I believe it is the sort known as the Italian grass snake and therefore not poisonous. The sun was going down before our task was completed, and looking towards the mountains we saw their snow-covered sides glowing in a deep rose hue. It was wonderful and almost unbelievable. We ceased our work to look at it but it only lasted a few minutes. Gradually the depth of colour grew paler and finally faded away, leaving the mountains cold and grim.

6.12.17

I was wise to lay in such a stock of tobacco before we left France. None has been issued to us since we left the train and none can be bought. Many of the fellows are smoking dried oak leaves. I am getting near the end of my store but there is still one quarter-pound tin in my valise at the Transport. I must get hold of that within the next day or so. Tobacco is more necessary than ever now that the pangs of hunger never get thoroughly appeased. We could eat at least half as much again as we get and then not be overfed. What we really crave for is bread; biscuits, even if we had them in abundance, cannot replace it. We feel perpetually empty.

8.12.17
Divisional Baths have been established at Selva so this afternoon Jamieson, Dickson and I went down and had our first bath for five weeks. The sun was hot and we sought the shady side of the road only to find it bitterly cold. In the village streets the snow has been churned into thin mud about two inches deep in which the native women splash about in bare feet. Saw an icicle almost as big and round as my body.

10.12.17
The Divisional Canteen has opened in Selva. McCormack and I went down to try and get some tobacco and anything in the eating line, but it was hopeless. After waiting 1½ hours in a queue the doors were shut — 'sold out'. MacDonald has scoured the country round on his motorcycle in an endeavour to buy food but only managed to get a small slice of polenta of which I had a share. The rations are so short that the cooks have to be most careful in issuing them — as long as every man gets the same there can

be no complaint. Biscuits, margarine, cheese and jam are supplied in bulk to each room of ten or twelve men and they have to divide it among themselves. Paterson and I are the ration drawers for our room and the dividing up has to be done with the most scrupulous accuracy. The men bring in their plates; we place them in a row on the floor and then carefully give each plate its share. Before allowing any plate to be removed we demand to know if any one has any objection; thus we avoid the possibility of any subsequent criticism or complaint. It is remarkable to observe how civilisation has produced qualities in men that are not possessed by other animals, notably forbearance and self-control. Our hunger is the hunger of wolves — it glistens from our eyes when we see any kind of food — the natural impulse is to snatch — we feel the pure animal rising in our breasts, but there is never the slightest suggestion of taking more than one's proper share. This, of course, is affected by the fact that we do get a certain amount of food each day and that tomorrow's rations are reasonably certain not to be worse than today's, but possibly better. We cannot say that we are suffering actual starvation but most assuredly we know the pangs of continual hunger. For breakfast we get a plate of porridge or a slice of bacon, for dinner, bully stew but no potatoes and once or twice we have had boiled rice. For tea a 1 lb tin of jam or ¼ lb cheese has to suffice for twelve men and this is where the 'doling out' has to be so exact.

14.12.17

Another big mail! Eight letters for me! But how am I going to answer them? None of us has been able to do much letter writing because of the extreme shortage of envelopes. I have managed to borrow four from MacDonald and have written two letters. The mail didn't bring many parcels. We have never before been in such urgent need of them and of course they don't arrive although we know that plenty have been despatched. For three whole weeks we had only two bread rations and they were Italian bread. Our own bakeries have now been established and we are getting a small ration of English bread for which we are devoutly thankful.

This climate is most bracing and invigorating and accordingly accentuates our hunger. The weather is beautiful and the view across the plain is marvellous. In the far distance we can see some tall towers and we like to think they are in Venice thirty miles away but I am more inclined to think they belong to Treviso. Looking over the plain with houses and villages and churches scattered over it as if shaken from a mighty pepper-box, we can picture humanity as midges toiling and moiling, striving and struggling — and all to what purpose? — while the mighty mountains before us, immovable and eternal, look down coldly and cynically, totally unaffected and unruffled by the petty struggles of the human beings on the plains.

15.12.17

We have been in the line a fortnight and tomorrow we are to be relieved. It seems a farce to talk about relief in warfare of this sort. There is a fair amount of aerial activity — the climate is conducive to it — but otherwise we seldom hear more than a dozen shells in the course of a day. We laugh and call it 'comic warfare'. On only one occasion have we had a touch of the real thing and that was a few days ago when the Austrians tried to get across the Piave both on our right and on our left, but they got thrown back so decisively that we don't think they will attempt any further attack for some time. They met French and British troops far different from the demoralised, disorganised and mutinous army that they had chased 125 miles from Caporetto. The bombardment began early in the morning and we were on the alert nearly all day. Directly after dinner, Glasspoole and I were sent to a vantage point from which we could look down on to our front line on the banks of the Piave. Our duty was to watch for the SOS signal which would go up if the enemy attempted to cross on our front. There was no shelter from the enemy's observation so we stood amongst thick undergrowth and kept still in the hope that we should look like tree trunks or oak saplings. Nothing happened for nearly two hours although we could hear the firing on both sides. Then suddenly a couple of shells burst just in front of us and made us look round hurriedly for any little bit of shelter, but we heard a voice in the distance calling my name, and looking towards the Wireless Station behind us we saw a man semaphore the 'CI' (i.e. 'come in'). We didn't wait for any more shells but hurried back to the Signal Office where we learnt that the attack had been vigorously repulsed. Another outstanding event which I have omitted to record under its proper date is the swimming raid across the river. We had only been in the line a few days when an officer and few men belonging to the Cyclist Corps one night swam across the swift, dangerous and icy cold Piave and penetrated 1000 yards into the enemy's lines, bringing back very useful information. It was a very courageous enterprise and only powerful swimmers could attempt it. It deserves recognition.

16.12.17
Returned to Selva for seven days in reserve. We are billeted in some large buildings attached to a fairly large house at the east end of the village. What the buildings are used for is more than I can tell. The entrance is like that of an old posting inn in England. We enter a door on the left of the archway and ascend a broad flight of stairs leading up to a very large chamber. I should think it is quite sixty feet long and thirty feet wide, with two archways on one side leading to another chamber about ten or twelve feet wide running the whole length of the large room. This smaller chamber contains straw and will be our sleeping quarters. A much smaller room near the top of the stairs is the Signal Office. It looks as if we shall be quite comfortable. Sent off four letters that I wrote yesterday.

17.12.17

Carrying out a tour of investigation, Fisher and I passed through a door that took us into the house proper. We found ourselves in a bedroom that had not been entirely denuded of its furniture. The people had evidently left in a hurry and had only taken the easily portable articles. In a chest of drawers we found a big pile of picture postcards of various parts of Italy, Austria and Switzerland. We shared them between us.

21.12.17

Much excitement all day long. All the men not on duty have been engaged in preparing and decorating the large room for our Christmas dinner. Some of them were out all the morning up on the hills getting holly, mistletoe and other foliage. Holly is very scarce but they managed to get a little. Tables and benches were obtained from somewhere and a stage, with draw curtains, erected at the far end. Oxley and McCormack brought back a good supply of turkeys, beef, pork, cabbages, potatoes, carrots, tinned fruit, biscuits, custard powder, tinned milk, beer, wine and syrupo, the latter being a descriptively named beverage indulged in by Italian teetotallers either for drinking or for quenching their thirst, I don't know which, but it is not much good for either. Also they brought nuts, oranges and apples. So we did well in the feeding line, and we deserved it for it was the first decent meal that we had had since we left France. We subscribed twelve lire (i.e. 6/-) per head but I think there is a surplus which will be refunded in some way or another. After the dinner came the concert. The interest centred on a sketch — a mere eight-minute skit on the Office particularly caricaturing Capt. Ainger (Staff Captain) and Mr Purvis (Signal Officer) and not omitting some of the NCOs. and men. I was the author, producer, stage manager, musical director and everything else all rolled into one. And it was a great success. All the Staff Officers came in to see it and they thoroughly enjoyed seeing two of their number parodied — indeed, Capt. Reah laughed till the tears ran down his cheeks. It was only three days ago that some of the men came to me with the request that I should write a sketch — so it has been pretty quick work. I have had to devote all my time to it. If I had had longer no doubt I could have improved it considerably, for there is plenty of material on which to exercise the gentle art of 'taking off'. But as it was, everybody was thoroughly amused and therefore I was quite satisfied. I must add that there was not the least display of jealousy or ill feeling among the men. Each man did the part allotted to him no matter how trivial or insignificant, and did it with great zeal and interest. They realised that it was impossible for all of them to be in the limelight; therefore they worked hand in hand for the common end.

25.12.17 Christmas Day
Today has been beautiful and very quiet. Our guns have fired a few rounds but the Italians and the Austrians have religiously abstained from any act of warfare. We live on rumours. The papers that we get are at least a fortnight old and it is extraordinary what remarkable rumours obtain currency.

Today they are strong on peace proposals from Germany. Hope springs eternal in the human breast and it is remarkable to observe how men clutch almost convulsively at the most improbable rumours if they point in the direction of their hopes and desires. But I place no faith in the lying jade. I cannot see the end of the war for another eighteen months and so I am labelled a pessimist. In reply I tell them that an optimist is a man who doesn't know what is in front of him.

26.12.17
Up this morning and on duty at 8 a.m. I had only just taken over when looking out of the window towards the line I saw an aeroplane come over. It was immediately followed by another and another and another until in less than one minute I had counted seventeen. They were flying so low, barely skirting the crest of the hills, that at first we naturally took them to be some of our own machines returning from a raid. But we soon saw the Iron Cross on their wings and suddenly all was excitement. Not a shot was fired at them because we had not had a second's warning of their approach and it was

impossible to train the machine guns on them before they had passed out of reach. They went over us not more than 200 feet up without dropping a bomb or firing a shot and scattered in all directions over the plain. For two hours or more we had a marvellous view of the most audacious air raid that I have ever heard of. From our position above the plain we could look down, not only on the country that was being bombed but also on the aeroplanes. Rifles and machine guns were firing briskly. Anti-aircraft guns could not get properly into action at such short range but they had a 'pot' at every opportunity. Bombs were dropping all over the place but without doing any serious damage as far as we could see; and every now and then one of the planes would burst into flames and crash to earth. Four or five within easy reach of unaided vision were entirely destroyed and two or three others were forced to land. Later in the day we learned that thirty-three machines had been engaged in the raid, twenty-seven Austrian bombers being escorted by six German fighters. Our 'bag' amounted to eleven machines, some of which were practically intact. A few pilots and observers were taken alive. It appears that the officers of the Austrian Air Force kept Xmas with a merry carousal lasting right through the night; and when, early this morning, orders to carry out the raid were received they were all pretty well drunk. This accounts for their recklessness. The main objectives were Corps HQ at Padova and the aerodrome at Forsalunga.

31.12.17

This morning I was ordered to relieve the Visual Station. Jamieson, who was already there, was to remain and I took Glasspoole and Cochran with me. We followed a cross-country track which will hardly be safe at night but which is much shorter than going by the road. Found Jamieson not at all well and presently he decided to 'go sick'. So I rang up Sgt Twycross and he sent McCormack to replace him. And now having arranged all the duties satisfactorily, we are settling down to make ourselves as comfortable as possible. Thus ends the year of grace 1917, a year of frightful agony and slaughter, of shattered hopes and broken lives; a year when humanity has sunk to incredible depths of inhumanity; a year that has brought tears to the eyes of the Recording Angel. But here are we, with our lot fallen in comparatively pleasant places, looking forward with an unquenchable hope to the New Year. Our souls have been scorched and seared by contact with Hell and we yearn for the healing oil of Peace.

that is what it looks like, but so far as I am aware there is no volcanic activity in the Alps. The next assumption, that it is undergrowth on fire, cannot be accepted as it does not spread but continues night after night in exactly the same place. So we are content with letting it remain a mystery.

17.2.18
Up betimes and marched halfway to Volpago. Here we halted for a few hours at a spot which is to be our Transport Quarters. Had a talk with one of the Dickeybirds who are going to rehearse my sketch when we come out of the line. I learnt incidentally that I lost an opportunity of playing the organ in the church at Ramon. This organ, a two-manual instrument, had not been played for two years because the organist was with the army and none of the remaining villagers knew how to play it. The priest looked among the British soldiers for an organist and I knew nothing at all about it. The Dickeybirds' pianist played it on one Sunday but he knows nothing about organs. However, he got through the service all right and this little act created a very favourable impression not only on the priest but on the community in general and resulted in the village hall being gladly handed over to the concert party.

About 3 o/c we once more got loaded up carrying blankets and overcoats as well as our standard equipment and started off for Road 14. My ankle was not painful but it was weak and made itself felt when we commenced to climb. Sgt Twycross took pity on me and allowed me to put my bundle of blankets on the wagon. It was a long pull up, the final stretch being so steep that the wagon had to take it at the run and my blankets were jolted off. We passed one of our howitzers hidden in a steep hollow. It must have been a rare job to get it there, but how they will get it out again without the assistance of an earthquake is more than we can imagine.

Our position appears to be very near if not quite the summit level of the Montello. Our quarters are a farmhouse situated on the lip of a large 'devil's punch bowl', one of the most perfect that I have seen. It is planted all round with vines and a wide spiral path leads to the bottom which is a flat space about sixty yards in diameter. In the sides of the bowl the 23rd Division have made a small but very fine tunnel with two entrances. It is large enough to shelter the whole of the Brigade HQ Staff in an emergency but there are only enough beds for the officers. It is the best piece of tunnelling that I have seen. Across the road in another dell is a small spring that will supply us with water. The cooks have established themselves in a shed near to it.

20.2.18

We are running a Visual Station in a house a few hundred yards away. The Italians have a Wireless Station in the same house and they charge their accumulators in a decidedly novel way. A little generator is driven by belting off the rear wheel of a pedal cycle suspended in a framework. For a certain period every day one of the Italian soldiers mounts the cycle and pedals furiously as if he were scratch man in a sprint.

21.2.18

From a warfare point of view, this spot is even more 'cushy' than Road 8. Each evening about half a dozen shells pass over us towards some of our batteries and this is all we have to worry us except aircraft during the day, but we are getting so indifferent to them that we hardly ever go to the trouble of taking cover. It is quite a holiday. Not far from us, in a small house, is an artillery observation post and Mennie, who has been there, tells me that the view across the Piave is wonderful. With the aid of powerful glasses they can see everything that goes on, even to the civilian women doing their washing. Once a day an Austrian battery dashes out from behind some low hills, swings round right on the bank of the river, fires half a dozen shots, and then bolts back again. From the field on the left of our billet we get a good view of the bridges that cross the river to Vidor. This is a point of honour and is held by picked Italian troops. I hope they will hold it well, for if the Austrians got across there our number would be up. George Thompson is making a painting of the view from this spot.

22.2.18

Early in the morning I had occasion to go into the billet and at my approach hundreds of rats scampered away in all directions. I shone my torch round the billet and it is certainly the most rat-infested building I have ever seen. They are much smaller than the Belgian variety but they make up for it in quantity.

Our troops carried out raids across the Piave in boats, guiding themselves by ropes that have been fastened between the numerous islands. The current is so strong that they have to keep a firm hold on the ropes or they would be washed away. They usually get one or two prisoners but so far I don't think we have suffered any casualties. The quietness of this front can be judged from the fact that our front-line troops wash and shave in the Piave which is as open to Fritz as it is to us. Also, Brigade Sports are being arranged to take place in our 'punch bowl', the level bottom being the arena while the troops will be comfortably seated round the sides. A boxing ring is already in course of construction. And this is being in the line!!

23.2.18

The weather is glorious — really too hot to exert oneself very much but this afternoon I went down to the ravine at the bottom of a slope where there is a copious well of icy cold water. I washed handkerchiefs, socks and a shirt and hung them in the sun to dry while I had a bath in a tin bowl. The sun was so hot that being naked was far from unpleasant, but oh! the water! It made my teeth chatter so I didn't dawdle over my bath. By the time I was dressed, my washing was dry enough to cart up to the billet. I'm getting pretty expert at washing but it's a job I should not care to earn my living at. Every job I think has its own particular soul or spirit — atmosphere, perhaps it may be called. So it is that sometimes I feel the washerwoman instinct creeping over me and I look at the weather and say, 'Ah, I think it will be a nice drying day, Mrs Glasspoole. P'raps you won't mind lending me your mangle for half an hour so as I can get these few things dried and ironed and put away before my old man comes 'ome which he do so 'ate to see washing about of a neevin.' Mrs Glasspoole replies suitably but I can't write it down. Well, today certainly has been a beautiful drying day and I felt like a man who has accomplished something when I took in the last pair of socks. About 5 p.m. a breeze suddenly sprang up — a thing so unusual as to attract attention — but it soon became almost a hurricane. It came straight from the mighty snowcapped mountains but the remarkable thing about it was that it was quite warm. Just as it was getting dusk we observed a bright light on the side of the mountains. It grew brighter and bigger and we made various speculations as to its nature. Then another appeared and another and another, four of them altogether. They were all in Fritz's territory and a good many miles away. Eventually we discovered that they were forest fires. The sides of the mountains are covered with bracken, undergrowth and trees and these being very dry, a slight spark is sufficient to set them aflame and the high wind did the rest until four enormous fires are raging over scores, perhaps hundreds, of square miles. It is now 10 o/c. I have taken a last look at the fires and this strange wind is still blowing fiercely.

Tonight there is a rumour of an impending move. I thought this sort of warfare was too good to last.

24.2.18
Last night's rumour has been confirmed and we have orders to pack up and leave here tomorrow. Evidently we are going out of the country and the usual rumours are abroad regarding Egypt, Salonika, France, Ireland and even England, but considering the way in which the Huns are making preparations in France I bet we land back in the Ypres Salient before long.

25.2.18
Yesterday we received slips of paper to stick in our pay books showing the new rates of pay dating from 29.9.17. Through getting Separation Allowance for my Mother I am 6d. a day better off as the government now pay the 6d. a day allotment that I made. Also I get 1d. a day war pay, having done over twelve months' active service. When I have completed the second year I shall have another rise of a penny. At present my daily rate is 2/3 [two shillings and threepence]

and I feel quite wealthy especially as it means picking up a lot of arrears. In the ordinary way, I am 200 lire (£5) in credit, and 7d. a day from 29 September up to today is £4.7s.7d. Now is the time that I should like a little trip to Rome or Florence or Milan — but no such luck — the betting is on Ypres or the Somme. It is a pity that we are leaving this country just as spring is coming in. We have lived through all the dead season and now Nature is just beginning to wake up. The dormant pulse of life is commencing to throb. Birds, butterflies and flowers — all are moving and stirring and there is the springtide coursing of the blood in our veins. No doubt many more kinds of birds will make their appearance, to say nothing of insects. Spiders have been numerous all through the winter and in great variety. I don't think I have seen the ill-famed tarantula but I have seen some very big ones, bigger than the palm of a man's hand. It is a messy job squeezing them!

I don't like spiders. They are interesting but have an evil, uncanny intelligence and the lady spiders eat their husbands.

26.2.18
Marched to Riese, a distance of about eight miles. Bought some postcards at a stall in the street and have solved the riddle of WPioX. In this little town Pope Pius X was born. Apparently he was of fairly lowly origin, judging from the size of the house in which he first saw daylight. On the house is a tablet

commemorating the event, supplemented by an appeal that visitors would regard the building as an object of historical interest and refrain from doing it any damage. In the street opposite the house is a monument to this pope surmounted by his bust.

27.2.18

The illustrated papers and magazines have recently published plenty of photographs and articles dealing with the extraordinary difficulties of mountain fighting particularly in the matter of transport. In one place I believe it takes twenty men to keep one man in the line. Naturally only real mountaineers can be employed in such positions. But today we have seen some of the genuine mountain fighters. Three or four of them looked rather like grizzly bears. They wore big white long-haired fur arrangements which covered them up completely except for just the front part of the face.

28.2.18

Today we have had little to do save prowl about waiting for orders. Bought two pairs of little wooden shoes or clogs, models of what the women wear. The local clog-maker has been very busy all day as half the troops wanted these little things to take away as souvenirs. The news is fairly definite that tomorrow we entrain for France.

Following the overthrow of the Tsar during the October Revolution, the new Bolshevik government speedily sought to end the nation's participation in the war. Negotiations between Russia and the Central Powers quickly brought about an Armistice in mid-December and although a final peace treaty (the treaty of Brest-Litovsk) was not signed until 3 March 1918, the Germans used the opportunity to begin withdrawing forces from the Eastern to the Western Front in order to launch a decisive campaign against the Allies in the spring.

With the Italian Front stabilised, and with overwhelming evidence that Germany was intending to embark on an all-out assault in France, Britain and France began to withdraw most of the Divisions sent to Italy in such haste in November of the previous year. The 41st Division, much to Martin's regret, was ordered to march and retrain for the Western Front.

In the first few days of March, Martin's diary largely retraces steps similar to those taken four months before by the Division. There are a number of observations of marginal interest about Verona, Milan and the long Alpine tunnels through which they passed back into France. He mentions the lack of gaiety as they cross the border once more, and he notes the train's passage through the Marne where the fighting had been so intense during the open days of warfare in 1914 and back again to Arras and then Ypres. Martin's travelogue back to France, though interesting, is perhaps not revealing enough to warrant inclusion here. For *this reason I have curtailed his notes to one fascinating incident that he jotted down as the train passed through northern Italy on 2 March.*

2.3.18

Presently the mountains rose up on both sides of us. They looked very stern and wild and forbidding and their tops were in the clouds. If it had been fine we would have enjoyed some magnificent scenery but we should have lost the wild grandeur of the snowstorms. We were pitying anyone who had to be out in that weather, when one of us noticed two little black figures struggling up the mountainside. We watched them for a long while and with the aid of field glasses made them out to be an Italian soldier followed by a priest holding up an umbrella. This I should think he found more of a hindrance than a help but he kept it above his head all the time. They followed a winding, tortuous path which we could not discern and they were the only animate creatures on the landscape. So it is no wonder that we immediately became intensely interested in them. They were fighting against fierce and unrelenting elements and our sporting instincts were roused. We almost got to betting as to how much further they would be able to go. A few buildings were visible here and there along their path but the travellers passed these and went winding onwards and upwards. Sometimes we lost sight of them behind great rocks and boulders and then we tried to guess just where abouts they would reappear. Still they kept going up and up until we feared that we should lose them in the clouds but at last they turned into a little tiny building, so small that we could scarcely pick it out, and we were glad to see them safely reach their destination for we felt that they were brave men to face the mountains in such weather. I wonder if they will ever know that they were watched, admired and cheered by a whole brigade of the British Army!

The sun was now sinking and we realised very forcibly that our little joy trip to Italy had ended. Our return to France was far different from our departure. Along the Riviera we were treated like heroes — we were cheered and worshipped by the crowds — but here there was only frost and snow and leaden skies, cold and cheerless and utterly lacking in sympathy. We knew we were back in France — we knew something of what we were going to meet — our gaiety was gone — we could sing 'Excelsior' no more. All we could do was to hum or whistle snatches of mournful music.

3.3.18
We travelled fairly well during the night for when we woke this morning we were some distance north of Dijon and were running through the Saône Valley. After the Alps, the scenery has not been very exciting; nevertheless it is not to be despised. It was fairly evident that we were travelling almost parallel with the fighting line and as the day wore on, evidence of the war

became more and more apparent and we could hear the booming of the guns. Yes, we know we are back in France again and our spirits have dropped accordingly.

4.3.18

We progressed in fitful spasms during the night. Consequently I woke up a number of times with the shaking and jolting of the train as it stopped and started. On one occasion we seemed to be at a busy spot judging from the noise and bustle of shunting and other railway operations. I rose up and opened the door to look out and something fell from the truck. As we were just on the move again I took no further notice but rolled up and went to sleep. In the morning my namesake Martin (who joined us only a few days ago) couldn't find his boots! I was sorry for him and at the first stop I went along to the Quarter Master to see if I could get another pair. But of course it was hopeless. All the Stores were securely packed in the wagons and could not be got at. We stopped in the sidings at Montdidier when we learnt that we were to detrain at a little place just beyond Amiens.

Arrived at Longeau where we put on our equipment and got out on to the platform only to be ordered back again as our destination had been changed. So on we went again travelling northwards until we reached Doullens. Here we detrained into about three inches of nice soft mud. Martin, minus his boots, was helped across to a motor lorry that was to take some of the stores to our billet. Then we marched off through the town and up the main Arras Road for some distance until we turned to the right and came to the little village of Halloy, seven kilometres from Doullens. This is a cheerless-looking hole; cold, dull, muddy and miserable.

7.3.18
The 11th RW Kents arrived in the village today and now the Brigade is complete once more, but there is a disquieting rumour abroad that one battalion in each brigade is to be disbanded as a part of a general scheme throughout the British Army to reduce the strength of each brigade to three battalions instead of four. The reason seems to be the shortage of reinforcements and the consequent difficulty of keeping battalions up to strength. There may also be some idea of increasing the mobility of Divisions. There is also some talk of the leave allotment being increased. There is some need, as while we were in Italy leave was almost restricted to special and urgent cases. Not a man from this section has had leave since last October so it is about time we started again.

9.3.18
Divisional orders today announce a big increase in the leave allotment so we all are a little more cheery although some of our chances are still pretty remote. Received letter and parcel from Elsie — jar of potted meat was smashed, but

otherwise it was OK and very welcome. All the runners attached to us have got the wind up over this disbandment rumour because whichever battalion is the unlucky one the runners belonging to it will have to return to their unit before it is split up and distributed as reinforcements all over France. Not a very entrancing prospect. Rumours on the matter are persistent but variable; sometimes they are strong on the Surreys, then they turn on to the Hants or the KRRs or the Kents, all perhaps within an hour, and spirits of the runners rise and fall accordingly. But there is nothing definite.

12.3.18
It is surprising how irritating it is when simple little questions or arguments arise which none of us can settle because we have no other source of information than our memories. *The Merchant of Venice*, which Elsie sent me, has just settled one grievous point, viz. who was in love with Portia. I was a bit hazy over most of the play but I said Bassanio. Hamilton stuck out that Bassanio eventually trotted off with Nerissa. He had got it into his head that although Bassanio and Portia were lovers in the early part of the play, the ring episode upset things and Bassanio married Nerissa. But I was correct and now I can gloat over Hamilton although really I have little right to do so for it was more of a guess than a feat of memory, but I don't admit that to Hamilton.

13.3.18

The death knell of the 11th Battalion Royal West Kent Regiment has been sounded. This morning orders were received that this is the unfortunate unit to be disbanded. And now the West Kent runners, Fisher, Granecome and Kirrage, are filled with misgivings, while all the others are heaving sighs of relief. Colonel Corfe (who is acting Brigadier while General Towsey is on leave) reviewed the battalion this afternoon.

14.3.18

General Lawford came and reviewed the Kents today, giving a little valedictory address explaining that it was no discredit to the battalion that it was being broken up. One battalion had to go and it was decided that where there was more than one battalion of the same regiment in the Division, the latest formed battalion must be the unlucky one. Accordingly in the other Brigades the 21st KRRC (123 Bde) and the 32nd Royal Fusiliers (124 Bde) are being disbanded. Endeavours are being made to retain our Kent runners but we are not certain that it can be achieved.

After the withdrawal of Russia from the war, the Germans transferred around a million men from the Eastern to the Western Front, giving them short-term but crucial numerical advantage. These men, backed by artillery, would pursue a campaign the broad strategic aim of which would be to divide the Allied forces, pushing the

BEF back on to its coastal ports, precipitating its defeat or at least forcing its retreat across the water.

Many of these men, fresh from the Russian Front, were well trained, battle-hardened and confident. It was Germany's moment to win the war before US troops arrived in such numbers as to irrevocably tip the balance against the Central Powers.

The Allies, in turn, had long anticipated such an attack. For two months they had prepared, utilising much that had been learnt in the previous years of fighting as well as introducing more recent innovations in defence that were designed to inflict as many casualties on the enemy as possible while preserving enough troops in reserve so as gradually to sap the enemy of his forward momentum and strength.

Nevertheless, there was a problem. The Commander-in-Chief, Haig, would be short of troops to meet the enemy. The protracted nature of the fighting, now in its fourth year, had driven a wedge between the senior command and many politicians at home, most significantly between Haig and the Prime Minister, Lloyd George. Fearing that Haig might use any reinforcements to launch his own spring offensive, Lloyd George had ordered that they should be held back in Britain and not in France, where they would be out of his control. Such a decision would ensure that when the Germans did attack, the British line would be more vulnerable than might otherwise have been the case. For the Germans, speedy infiltration would be the key to success, pushing some of the best trained and equipped German soldiers deep into Allied lines to sow confusion. Allied strongpoints would be largely ignored in the rush to storm the entire trench system, while mopping-up parties would later be used to clear up any remaining resistance by men who were surrounded and deep in enemy territory.

The date for the attack was 21 March, an important fact gleaned from German prisoners captured in raids a few days beforehand. Even so, the ferocity of the attack when it came was overwhelming. At 5.30 a.m., after a short whirlwind bombardment had softened up the Allies' forward trenches, the Germans advanced, helped by a thick fog that hid the attackers until they were almost on top of the British trenches. The fighting was intense and it was fluid. The British, compelled to retreat, often in headlong flight, were incapable of holding their position for any length of time although they inflicted heinous casualties on the German army, losses the Germans could ill afford.

March and April produced some of the darkest moments for the Allies and in particular for the British Army. Less than a month after his comfortable sojourn in Italy, Jack Martin was thrown into the maelstrom, his diary adequately reflecting the insecurity and pandemonium of the time.

17.3.18

The German attack is expected very shortly; consequently a 'nervy' atmosphere is commencing to make itself felt. To stir up our brutal instincts and passions we have been treated to a morally disgusting harangue by a Major of the Physical Jerks Department. The whole Brigade was marched out to a field a few kilometres away where we squatted down in a hollow while the blood-red Major (straight up from the base) delivered his oration in a strikingly melodramatic manner. He endeavoured to make us 'see red' and it is a matter for sad reflection that civilisation should come to such a sorry pass. The authorities apparently think that the civilian-soldier is too soft hearted and gentle so it is necessary to raise the spirit of Cain in him. The whole speech was utterly disgusting and I am sorry to think that England should consider such a thing necessary. It was revolting and I believe I could better have withstood a dose of the abject platitudinous piffle that deals with the 'nobility and righteousness of our cause', 'the honour of dying for England' and 'Remember Belgium'.

18.3.18

Rumours as to the German attack have been many and varied but a telegram from GHQ says it will be on 20th or 21st, most probably the latter. I have just been on duty with Bill Rogers. There was very little to do and I intended writing a few letters, but that was impossible, for

Rogers was talking and telling yarns all the time. He is a Lance Corporal of the Surreys and has been attached to us ever since the Division came out. A Londoner, he is almost a typical cockney, extremely loquacious and with a fund of humorous reminiscence which seems to have no end. Once get him fairly wound up (by no means a difficult job) and he will keep going all night; we have whiled away many a weary hour listening to his stories. In 'civvy' life he is a specialist in poultry, fish, eggs and milk, so he has been of great assistance at our Christmas feasts. Although very voluble he isn't noisy like Davidson and it is very seldom that he tries to sing. Most of his tales are concerned with the inner life of fish, poultry and dairy businesses. Some of them have prompted me to suggest that he writes a book on 'How to make Money on a Milk-round' — circulation to be strictly confined to the trade. So long as he can get an audience he is perfectly content. It is quite immaterial whether they can understand him or not, so, on the Montello one day, we were not surprised to find him talking volubly to a small party of Italian soldiers (who could not understand a single word) about Lloyd George and the prospects of peace. 'Ah,' he said, 'you don't know him. He's one of those fellows who if the Germans threw up their hands and cried, 'We give in, we've had enough: you can have France and Belgium and all the Colonies as well, and you can have the whole of Germany too' would answer, 'Oh no you don't, we'll fight you for it.' ' Davidson, by the way, is not so confident of an early peace as he was in Italy. There he was a very strong peace optimist despite several very severe reversals in that quite a number of his dates for the end of the war had come and gone and left us just as uncertain as before. But the German attack looming immediately before us provides a very efficient corrective to the unduly optimistic views that were induced by the blue skies, clear air and gentle warfare on the Italian Front.

19.3.18
There is little to think or talk about except the imminence of the German attack. Gradually we have been making the preparations necessary for our part, and as a final touch we were treated to a false alarm this afternoon for the purpose of seeing how quickly we could turn out with wagons packed and everything ready for the march. As it was we were packed up and all in line in a remarkably short time, and the Brigadier was very pleased. But we didn't tell him that we knew what was coming, four or five hours before the alarm was sounded. I am on night duty tonight and, judging from the tone of one or two telegrams that have passed, it is pretty certain that the attack will commence on the 21st.

21.3.18
Great German Attack. Although at Halloy we were well behind the lines, the sudden and

terrible thunder of innumerable guns woke me at dawn. The long-expected German Advance had commenced. It had been foretold long before we left Italy, the date being fixed about the end of March or beginning of April as, in the words of Sir Douglas Haig, 'the initiative will then have passed into the enemy's hands'. Why it should be allowed to pass is a little more than I can understand at present. But this is no time to dwell on whys and wherefores. We are in the soup and we've got to get out of it. Gaiety and mirth have been dwindling of late, and what merriment there was as we rose this morning had little spontaneity about it. But the British soldier in the mass never gets downhearted. So when late in the afternoon we were formed up and marched away, we kept our spirits up with singing and laughing. We went along the main Arras Road to Saulty, a distance of eight miles. Here were some of our long-range guns and we felt that we were getting back into the fighting arena once more. Detachments of the Chinese Labour Corps (affectionately known as 'Chinks') were straggling down the road, no two men dressed alike and all of them carrying a miscellaneous assortment of odds and ends, such as field kettles, tins, saucepans, picks, axes etc. They dearly love to get hold of some item of the British soldiers' clothing or equipment. The fit doesn't matter — jackets, trousers, puttees, even if it is only one puttee they will wear it with pride. But they are mighty cowards. The firing of one of our own guns nearby was quite enough to set them scuttling down the road like frightened rabbits. At nightfall we entrained and understood that our immediate destination was Méricourt on the Somme, a few miles behind Albert and a place that we had known in 1916. We were uncomfortably crowded in the trucks and could only squat down with our knees up under our chins. Of course all leave has been stopped.

22.3.18
Horribly cramped, I only doze fitfully all night yet it is surprising how soundly some men can sleep in any position. One by one they woke up and stretched, kicking and pushing all the other fellows around them. It was broad daylight when we opened the doors and found that already we were beyond Méricourt and were actually passing through Albert. We crawled along until we reached Achiet-le-Grand where we detrained at 8.30 a.m. There was little hope of any breakfast but fortunately there was a large Expeditionary Force Canteen adjoining the railway. Here we bought tea and cake and cigarettes and tobacco. In a little time we were ordered to fall in as we were going straight into the line. All this part of the country was held by Fritz before the Somme Offensive in 1916 and now he is bent on getting it back again, and a little bit more if he can. Naturally there is much evidence of warfare both past and present, to say nothing of the possibilities of the future. The whole Signal Section and Brigade Headquarters Staff were lined up and inspected by General Towsey who carefully noted

that each man had his full supply of ammunition and iron rations. It was a rather impressive inspection with shells bursting less than a mile away and all the multitudinous sounds of warfare rattling in our ears. There was no particular ceremony about the business; it seemed more like a fatherly interview and there is no doubt that General Towsey felt considerable anxiety for our welfare. He always has had a high regard for his Signallers and now it was very evident. The inspection was brief as we were awaiting orders to relieve one of the Divisions that has been in the line ever since the attack commenced yesterday morning. I don't know how far the Germans advanced yesterday but we have heard pretty definitely that since they resumed the attack at dawn today they have come over ten kilometres, a rather terrifying rate when compared with our advances in the Ypres Sector last year, where we measured our territorial gains in yards. It also appears that the Germans are coming over equipped to stay, each man carrying a spare pair of boots and two water bottles, one containing water and the other coffee. And this is in addition to his ordinary equipment and extra ammunition.

After the inspection we ate what bully beef and biscuits we could get and then General Towsey decided that only the next two shifts of men for duty should be taken into the line. The rest were to remain with the Transport until they were wanted. My luck is in, for I was one of the last men on duty at Halloy. When the others had gone forward we looked around and found a Nissen hut wherein we installed ourselves, and before long the cooks had made some tea. At nightfall the firing slackened a bit as, apart from the weariness of the troops, it is impossible to continue an advance in the dark. We felt that we were reasonably secure for the night, so, covered with our overcoats, we went to sleep.

23.3.18
Up soon after daybreak as we knew not what was before us. The cooks were preparing breakfast, bacon was frying and tea was brewing, when we received orders to retire immediately as the Germans had resumed their alarming advance. Tea and bacon were thrown overboard, the wagons were roped up, and off we marched to Buchanan Camp (a distance of three miles) lying between Achiet-le-Grand and Achiet-le-Petit but nearer the latter. This is a tolerably large camp with several rows of good huts. Here we made ourselves as comfortable as possible, even managing to get blankets from the Quarter Master. In the afternoon, just outside our huts, we saw a parade of what was left of a battalion of the Essex Regiment. All that had come back were the Colonel, one NCO and thirty men. The Major also was there but from what I heard he had been left behind when the battalion went into the line. First of all the Major called the roll and went through other necessary routine business. Then the Colonel came forward and addressed the men. He was visibly affected and had difficulty in delivering his little speech, for emotion was half choking him and tears were rolling down his cheeks. He

was tall and big, with a square jaw and a hard-cut face that had probably never felt a tear before. His words had a simple nobility and directness about them and I shall remember his speech as one of the most considerable that I have ever heard. We were not surprised afterwards to hear him spoken of as a brave and splendid man. I do not know who he was but I shall not forget him.

24.3.18

This morning we managed to get a good breakfast and then, as it seemed unlikely that we should be moved for an hour or two, Davidson and I walked up to the German Cemetery at Achiet-le-Petit. There had been a hospital here in 1916 and amongst the enemy graves we found one to a British Tommy who had died from wounds and one to a Flying Corps Officer whose plane had been shot down. Returning, we were met by a continuous stream of retiring troops, fatigued almost to the point of absolute exhaustion, staggering along hardly knowing where they were going. Hot, tired horses pulling guns of all calibres while, on the gun limbers, artillerymen, who had been firing their guns for three whole days and nights, slept a precarious slumber in the continual danger of being jolted into the road and being trampled by the team immediately behind.

At the camp we heard that the Canteen at Achiet-le-Grand had been abandoned. The Corporal in charge had taken all the money and hurried back, leaving the Canteen to the mercy of the troops. In a very short time it was utterly ransacked and I daresay it held at least £2000 worth of stuff. We were among the less fortunate in the scramble but some of our fellows brought back two cases of whisky and numerous boxes of biscuits and cigarettes. From the top of the rise near the camp we could see the bursting shells approaching nearer and nearer but we did not get the order to move until the shells were dropping in the camp. One went clean through one of the huts that we had been in. It was getting dusk by the time we had loaded up and were ready for the road again.

Incidentally, the Quarter Master jettisoned a whole lot of stores and paraphernalia, including all the 'props' of the Dickeybirds Concert Party, amongst which was the sketch I wrote for them in Italy. So that doesn't look like ever being performed.

Along the road a little way, we passed a big howitzer that had just been got into position and was beginning to open fire again. The roads were so congested with traffic at this point that we had to make tracks across some fields only to get our feet entangled with telephone wires. These were dangerous for the horses but we had no mishap and eventually turned into a large field on the left of the road. It was 10 p.m. before we got the transport settled and looked round for some sort of shelter for ourselves. But there was none. QMS Cass doled us out with two blankets each. Wrapping these round us, we lay down on the grass against a long, low mound, the slope of which formed something of a pillow. Tired, but very thankful it was a fine night, we were not long in dropping off to sleep. I sent field postcards to Mother and Elsie but Corporal Smith (the post Corporal) does not hold out much hope of their early despatch.

25.3.18

The opening of the barrage at dawn woke us and we found our blankets and heads covered with white frost. There was a certain expectancy in the air and we rolled up our damp blankets and had a hurried breakfast. The traffic on the road was increasing every minute and soon it began to flow over into the fields on either side. Hundreds of wounded men were struggling to get back. All kinds of wagons and limbers and civilian carts had been requisitioned to carry them back to hospital but the quantity of transport was insufficient; consequently, all those who could walk or even only hobble had to do so. It was a painful spectacle but we had little time in which to bestow pity for we were marched out on to the road while our transport was ordered to make its way across the fields towards Ayette. We had no idea where we were going and I don't think Mr Edgar had either. We had only gone a few paces down the road when a gaudy colonel dressed in a regulation tunic but with light blue trousers with red stripes galloped up and stopped us. 'Where are these men going?' he demanded. 'Down this way,' stammered Mr Edgar. 'About turn!' yelled the gaudy colonel, 'Follow me!' and away we had to go, heading straight for the line.

The prospect was not very pleasing and besides we had heard some strange tales of Germans dressed as British officers penetrating into our lines and trying to take command of parties of our men. So we viewed this queerly dressed officer with suspicion although from what transpired there is little reason to doubt that he was British. I was in the middle of the party (a very mixed lot from all our battalions) and after going less than a hundred yards I looked round and saw Davidson, Rogers, Paterson and Jamieson calmly drop out and cut across the field in the direction taken by our transport. 'A good example,' I thought, 'is worth following, and in any case this is no place for me.' So I promptly followed them. By this time the fields as well as the roads were covered thick with a heterogeneous mass of all conceivable kinds of transport, guns and men, and it was not an easy matter to find our own transport. Fortunately it had not been able to get along very fast and when we found it we distributed ourselves among the wagons, avoiding any suggestions of congregating as there seemed to be a number of freelance officers knocking about whose duty was to gather up all the odds and ends of humanity who were not engaged in some duty or other, and form them into scratch parties or 'composite' battalions and lead them off up the line. They are to be avoided at all costs for they are nobody's darlings, and apart from getting the dirty work they are in a hopeless position in regard to rations, doctors, ambulances etc. There are not many men made of such heroic fibre that they would willingly join a composite party in a stunt like this. We crawled along a lane that led us past Divisional HQ into Ayette. In the village there was a tremendous block of traffic at the crossroads. We halted for nearly an hour but could not get over. Then fresh orders were received and with difficulty we turned round, passed out of the village and were soon travelling along a road that we had almost to ourselves. And so we came to Gommecourt but Divisional HQ were before us and had installed themselves in the ruins of the chateau. The village had been knocked all to pieces in 1916 and notice boards outside the ruins of the church and at the entrance to an old German dugout proclaimed, in French, that the authorities were preserving these as permanent memorials of the Great War.

Near the chateau we turned into a field where we anticipated spending the night. McCormack and I scrounged the countryside and brought back some sheets of corrugated iron wherewith to make some sort of shelter while the cooks made some tea. Dickson, Blakeway and the other fellows who had followed the gaudy colonel now returned. They had been led into a hastily constructed trench to stop the German Cavalry which was expected to break through. Nothing of the sort happened, however, and soon they were left to themselves. With no one to command them and not having the vaguest idea of what they were required to do, and also being very hungry, they all decided to vacate the trench and try and find the transport. Night was falling and we were trying to build a shelter when we received further orders to get on the move again. The moon was hidden by clouds as we trekked through Fonquevillers to Souastre. Just beyond this village we were put into a field for the night. It was now drizzling with rain and a night in the open was not an attractive prospect, but with the help of some iron stakes and barbed wire we made a roof of blankets.

26.3.18
There was a tense feeling in the air this morning and strange rumours were flying about. At 8.30 a.m. orders were received that every available man was to be sent to some unnamed spot. Only NCOs and the actual drivers were to remain with the transport. Capt. Reiner decreed that all the Signals must go, so we were issued out with iron rations and a double quantity of ammunition, and under Lieut. Edgar we passed back through the village and up the road leading to Sailly-au-Bois. There was an alarming stir at Div. HQ in Souastre — Staff Officers were dashing about furiously and gallant NCOs who had never been in the firing line looked livid and scared as if they did not know what to do. We were not left long in doubt as to the cause of the commotion, for we had barely got clear of the village when we met men hurrying from the opposite direction. Lorries, horse transport and men on foot all seemed anxious to get past us. Then we met some who called out as they hurried by, 'Don't go up there, you bally fools — Fritz is in the next village!' Mr Edgar halted

us, ordered us to load rifles and fix bayonets, and was surprised to find that RE Signals do not carry bayonets. Then we were lined across the field on the right of the road and quickly the word was passed round that the German Cavalry had broken through and might be upon us at any moment. Except for a few yards of trench there was no shelter for us at all and only one of our party had an entrenching tool. We borrowed it in turn and scraped grave-shaped holes to lie in, building the earth up in front of us to form some slight protection. Other men were doing the same thing in front of us and behind us and within half an hour there were fourteen lines of resistance drawn right across the country. We kept our eyes on the horizon and waited. It was a most horrible wait. Some there were in our line who were faint-hearted — but there was no RE among them — and crept back to the security of a little sunken lane behind us. I heard Paterson say to Jamieson, 'So much for them, but I have been put here, and here I am going to stop until an officer orders me to move.' The grim determination was heartening.

The ground fell away slightly in front of us and then rose to a long line of low hills on the horizon. For three hours we lay and watched the skyline but nothing German made any appearance. A number of horsemen came over but they were British and soon we were talking to a Sergeant of Artillery who told us definitely that the rumour was false. We got up and stretched ourselves, and breathed freely once more. It is positively extraordinary how this rumour spread over such a vast expanse of country in such an incredibly short time — just like a big puff of wind. But it is equalled by the extraordinary organisation which flung fourteen lines of resistance across the country in little more than the same number of minutes. Now we only had to wait for orders, so we wandered about a bit to stretch our legs and get ourselves warm, for the wind was rather cold. Presently I noticed men coming from the direction of the village carrying armfuls of socks, cap comforters, gloves, etc. Others had new caps, tunics, greatcoats, breeches, trousers and boots. It soon appeared that Div. HQ had scuttled off in such a hurry that they left all their stores behind them. I am pretty well equipped so there was no need for me to join in the looting. All this time the scene behind us was amazing. The contour of the land dipped and rose again so that we had a view of several roads leading out of Souastre. These were absolutely choked with transport so that nothing could move for at least four hours. Every time we looked back, the same wagons were visible in exactly the same places. The afternoon was well advanced before they made any definite move. At 4 o/c we were called off and put into a barn on the edge of the village. Of course there were no rations so we started to scrounge. At the deserted Div. HQ we found all we wanted — tea, sugar, tins of milk, bullybeef, 'maconochies', biscuits and potatoes, together with the necessary field kettles to cook them in. The stores and billets gave unmistakeable evidence of the alacrity with which the Div. HQ evacuated its quarters. Blankets were lying in heaps just as the fellows had bundled out of them, and not many of the men had stopped to put their puttees on. Soap, cleaning and shaving tackle and all manner of personal odds and ends had been left behind in the scramble. We cooked a good meal of stew and tea, then collected as many blankets as we wished (I had six) and made ourselves comfortable in the loft over the barn. Meanwhile, some rough spirits of the 51st (Highland) Division had broken into the farmhouse and thoroughly looted it. Everything they wanted, they took: all else they smashed and destroyed, even tearing doors off hinges and breaking up the furniture and tearing the women's clothing to pieces. The farmer, his wife and daughter had locked the place up in their alarm earlier in the day and had gone to some friends in the village. What a nice return for them! It was not till all the damage was done (including running off all the wine from the barrels) that an officer was found to call the men to order.

27.3.18

The remnants of yesterday's tea served us for breakfast and about 9 o/c we marched to Bienvillers. Along the road there was abundant evidence of the mighty scramble the Transport had yesterday. A lot of it had forsaken the roads and taken to the fields in order to get back somehow or other. Arriving in Bienvillers, we found the place thronged with 122nd Brigade troops and, before we reached the centre of the little town, Sgt Twycross met us and we learnt that the Brigade had been withdrawn from the line during the night. What the next move was to be was not known but we were ordered to carry on with the Transport, so away we went to Berles where we found them in a field at the end of the village. We were welcomed by Davidson who fetched out a parcel he had just received and regaled us with shortbread and biscuits.

28.3.18
The Brigade has been suddenly ordered back into the line again. We had expected to be kept out for at least a week in order to collect reinforcements for we have lost very heavily. It is fairly evident, however, that we shall not be in for long. Indeed, it is impossible for the Brigade, in its sadly depleted condition, to do much in the way of fighting. Enticknap is missing. He was last seen amid heavy shelling near Bucquoy.

29.3.18
On to Couin where we arrived about midday. This area is strongly populated by the Brigade of Guards and their excessive discipline is very evident. Very 'posh', and very shiny and not often in the line but when they are, they make themselves felt. I have heard that near Achiet-le-Grand they went over in a counter-attack as cool as going on parade.

We are billeted in some farm buildings near the chateau. Troops have been here before, as wire-netting beds have been erected in one of the lofts; so we shall be reasonably comfortable tonight.

30.3.18
We have found a place in the village where we can buy candles and coffee but not much else. The 'fag issue' today has produced some tobacco for which I am grateful. The weather has been fine and not having much to do, albeit in a continual state of expectancy, I wrote a fairly long letter to Elsie. Dashing about the neighbourhood in a big car is a ferocious looking Major of the Guards with six wound stripes, his arm always resting on the side of the car for display purposes.

1.4.18
Expecting our moving orders all day but they did not come until the afternoon. So we had a hurried tea and then marched off to Marieux where we arrived after dark and were tightly squeezed into one end of a hut, leaving the remainder vacant as the Brigade is coming out of the line during the night and the other fellows must have room to lie down.

2.4.18
At 3 a.m. we were awakened by the noisy arrival of the Brigade but in about an half an hour the lot of us were asleep again. There was no hurry

in getting up as we were not due to move till after dinner. The German Advance in this quarter seems to be fairly well stemmed and we are breathing a little more freely. Sgt Lunn says that we are bound for the Ypres Salient again.

4.4.18
It was still dark when we were bundled out of the train at Poperinghe and tramped through the deserted streets of the dingy little town to a large building that has the appearance of being a warehouse or store. Here we dumped ourselves down to slumber but it was too cold for me to sleep, so Cheesman and I wandered out into the town. It was now daylight and the natives were beginning to stir. We have had very little bread lately so we were quite pleased when we found a baker's shop. We went into the kitchen, made ourselves comfortable by the fire and drank coffee. The baker told us that they were forbidden to sell bread to British troops, but nevertheless we both came away with a loaf tucked under our greatcoats.

6.4.18
This morning, a party of us went off to what was once a brewery but which now, unblushing, proclaims itself to be a Delousing Station. There we had a good bath, which we desperately needed, while our clothes were fumigated, which they, also, desperately needed. Later I wrote another batch of letters. The 41st Division has

been specially mentioned in one of Sir Douglas Haig's despatches concerning the operations on the Somme.

7.4.18
Last night orders were received for us to move up into the line today and this morning I was told to take charge of a relay station in Ypres. So with Glasspoole, Cochran, Chappell and Dagnall, I set off through Poperinghe and straight along the Ypres Road. On the way we had to find the location of the Transport and deliver a message to Capt. Mowat. To save time, I sent Cochran forward on a cycle to do this little business but of course he was a failure. So I did the job myself. At the YMCA Hut near Brandhoek we called a halt for refreshments and then carried on through Vlamertinghe to Ypres. Our directions were vague; all we knew was that we had to take over a Signal Office somewhere in the Ramparts. There was no shelling as we passed straight through the ruined town until we came to the Menin Gate — here the Ramparts ran right and left — we took the left and were lucky in soon striking the Signal Office in a dugout. The 99th Brigade had cleared out but had left a few written directions to guide us in joining up our instruments. Just across the road are some recently erected huts which seem to declare that Ypres isn't quite such a Hell as it was before the Passchendaele stunts last year, but they don't seem to have been used a great deal.

9.4.18

Fritz leaves Ypres alone during the day but gives it some attention during the night. We have been able to explore the town a bit by daylight but as soon as darkness falls it's advisable to keep under cover. One of the first shells over tonight broke the line connecting us with the Division on our right. Before going out to repair it, I rang up Sgt Twycross in order to find out who was responsible for keeping it in order. He said it was the duty of the other Division so I took no further interest in it. I wasn't sorry as Fritz was giving us rather more attention than was pleasant. Presently in came two linemen; they had found the break just outside our dugout and had mended it. They stopped and yarned until about 10 o/c and then, as the shelling was less severe, they took their departure.

10.4.18

Sgt Twycross rang up this morning and gave instructions for Glasspoole to make his way to Zuytpeene for the purpose of undergoing a special signal course. So he packed up and was away before noon. No one is coming in his place and that means that Cochran and I will have to run the office between us all night as well as all day. Rather exhausting if it's going to last long.

11.4.18

Last night I left Cochran to take the first night shift (from 10 till 3) but before 11 I got up and went into the Signal Office and found him fast asleep. I talked to him very sweetly and I think he remained awake all right for the rest of his shift — any rate, he was quite up to time in rousing me at 3 a.m. The Brigade is in a very unpleasant quarter. The country is an expanse of soft mud and to slip off the duckboards means getting half drowned. In addition they have been subjected to continual shelling ever since they took over.

After dinner, acting in accordance with instructions received during the morning, we left our little dugout and proceeded to rejoin the Brigade at Wieltje. Near St Jean a railway crosses the road and our passage was blocked by a long train of trucks. A noise and a rattle in front of us attracted our attention and we saw a two-horse Artillery limber rushing headlong down the road straight towards the train. The driver was doing all he knew to pull up the runaways, but they had got the bits between their teeth and it looked a dead cert for a nasty accident. But the driver lost neither his head nor his seat and he very cleverly managed to pull his team sharp right along the railway track by the side of the train and then, plunging into about two feet of mud, the mad career was checked.

12.4.18

The day has been fine and as there was practically no shelling in the neighbourhood we spent most of the time out in the open. In the afternoon Johnny Aitken was wounded in the knee and has been taken to hospital. As the evening approached we gathered in the saps and prepared to depart. We had all got our kit on and were climbing up the stairs when Fritz started on a terrific bombardment, blowing in one of the entrances but not causing any casualties. This delayed us nearly an hour, but when we set off everything was quiet. Crossing the country we reached the Ypres — Zonnebeke Road and continued towards the latter place until we reached Jump Dugout, a small but very substantial German pillbox. It is uncomfortable, dark and stuffy but its solidity gives us a sense of security.

14.4.18

The empty quietness of the neighbourhood is weird. The silence is only broken by an occasional shell although from the south there is a continual heavy roar. The Germans have made considerable advances in the direction of Hazebrouck and Bailleul and they appear to have captured Ploegsteert. Now that I am back with Brigade I am able to see the official reports as they come through. Our pillbox is fitted with a periscope but there is no need to use it for it is quite safe to go outside. I don't think we have had a shell fall within 300 yards of us since we have been here.

15.4.18

Last night we sent a lot of stuff back on the Transport wagon that brought up the rations. We only kept what is needed for today as the evacuation is to take place tonight. All the innumerable details have been arranged, consequently most of the day has been spent in waiting and watching. The whole area is to be entirely cleared by 3 a.m. So, shortly . . .

16.4.18

. . . after midnight Lally came up with the limber and we loaded up the remainder of the Stores and finally closed down the Signal Office with the assistance of an axe and a couple of hammers. We smashed everything that we could not take away — it was sheer wanton destruction that we could enjoy. McCormack put his heart and soul into it with a vigour that won a round of applause. Leaving a party of Field Coy REs to blow up the dugout and so give it the final coup-de-grâce, we lined up on the road and commenced our retirement. It was an eerie trek through the still and almost silent night. On all sides of us was the shell-blasted mud of Flanders, familiar enough in all conscience, but now in a new guise. It was lifeless. Passing the British Cemetery at Potijze, we entered Ypres by the Menin Gate. In the first cold glimmerings of a cheerless dawn the naked, shivering ruins of the old town rose up stark and grizzly around us. The shattered tower of the Cloth Hall gazed at us silently with a reproachful wondering. Were we deserting it for ever? It was a question none of us could answer.

17.4.18

Had a mediocre bath at Vlamertinghe Brasserie this morning, and again spent much time in writing letters. The Germans have captured Hazebrouck and Meteren but from the reports it appears that the attack in that quarter has just about spent itself, which is a relief as much more of it would cut us off entirely. The Somme Offensive seems to have exhausted itself and so Fritz is trying his hand at something less ambitious.

18.4.18

Capt. Ainger and Capt. Reah have been taken to hospital suffering badly from gas. They shared a gas shell between them a few nights ago when they were making arrangements for the evacuation. The weather is pretty dismal. For several days it has been dull and cloudy, and today there is a cold wind accompanied by drizzling rain. Still, there are plenty of signs of spring in the budding hedgerows (what is left of them), and in bright intervals, birds sing and chirrup gaily. They aren't worried at all by the beastly war and these are times when I feel quite envious of them. Still, I suppose they have their little feuds and strifes, but they manage to keep pretty merry withal.

able to summon enough men and materials to mount an offensive of any consequence. They had battered away at Allied lines in March, then April, then May and even into June, switching the direction of attack in the increasingly desperate hope that one more push might bring about the collapse that they had so earnestly desired in the Allied resolve to fight. But there was no collapse: although at times the Allied cause looked bleak, they nevertheless held the Germans at bay, inflicting like-for-like casualties that the Allies could countenance but the Germans, increasingly outgunned, could not hope to lose and then replenish. By August, it was clear that, with American troops entering the conflict in greater and greater numbers, and with British and French forces about to take to the offensive once more, the Germans could do little but hold the ground they stood on. On 8 August even this proposition was fully undermined by an Allied offensive that tore through German lines and took such large numbers of prisoners that the German High Command privately acknowledged the war was lost. It was, as they later said themselves, the Black Day for the German army. From that moment, the German forces began an inexorable retreat, first across the battlefields they had fought so hard to win earlier that year, then later across the open, unspoilt lands that had lain behind their positions for almost the entire war. The last great defensive position, the Hindenburg Line, was stormed at the end of September and there remained little to do but to fall back, perhaps as far as Germany and the Rhine itself. The question was only when the Germans might sue for peace.

31.8.18
A day of excitement. From the official reports that have been coming through, it appears that Fritz has evacuated Kemmel Hill and the line that we held throughout July and August. The 124th Brigade were in the line awaiting the relief that would enable them to come back to this area but they have been ordered to keep in touch with the enemy and we have to go back to join them. So our three weeks' rest has promptly been reduced to three days. We have to move from here tomorrow morning and there has been considerable rushing about since the order was received to get everything packed up as far as possible.

2.9.18
So far as we are concerned the military situation is somewhat obscure and we have spent this day in hanging about waiting for orders that did not arrive until the evening. And now we know that tomorrow we go into the line almost on the jolly old St Eloi front.

3.9.18
My birthday — and some birthday too! The busiest one I have ever spent. When we were

ready to march off, Sgt Twycross told me to go across to the Transport (at the next farm) taking Dagnall with me as a runner. I was to try and establish communication with Brigade as soon as they got into the line. All the morning and afternoon I was trudging about here and there, backwards and forwards, 'tapping in' on every line I could find. I discovered a Test Box but none of the terminals produced a line that was of any use to me. By teatime I was tired out and just wanted to lie down and rest but a message came down from Brigade that I was to take a cycle and meet a runner who would be leaving Brigade with an important message about 6 p.m. Lally also had to follow with some stores on the limber and I told Dagnall to accompany him. The countryside seemed remarkably quiet as I approached Reninghelst. This little town, of more or less happy memories, was practically deserted. It has been very badly knocked about and of course no civilians have lived in it since last April. Nearby I met Morris with the all-important message but as I was now within a few yards of Brigade I decided to go and see the boys; but I didn't stop long. Before I got as far back as Reninghelst I met Lally and Dagnall. Giving the message to Dagnall to take back on the cycle, I returned to Brigade HQ with Lally, unloaded the stores and had a look in some of the dugouts. A few shells were coming over but nothing to get alarmed about yet the mules were a bit restive so Lally was anxious to make a move.

When we had got back to Ouderdom I

suddenly remembered a message that I ought to have delivered to Brigade from Capt. Mowat so back we had to go once more. When we reached the Transport Lines it was five minutes to midnight and I was dead beat. Earlier in the day we had dumped our kit in the Quarter Master's hut as we could find no other billet, and here I now fetched out my blanket and rolled myself up in it. The mail had come up while I was out and there was a pile of letters and parcels for me. Lying in my 'kip' I read the letters and then fell asleep.

7.9.18
A couple of days ago Sgt Pragnell came back from leave and brought up in a wagon several dozen bottles of beer for the Officers' Mess. It seemed a pity to let them go straight up the line and 'Praggy' wasn't anxious to go on any further that evening. So we unloaded the bottles and stood them in the Quarter Master's hut where we could keep our eye on them. Somehow or other that evening there didn't seem much to do after dark so we had plenty of time to keep our eyes on the bottles and see that none was stolen. And that is how the little conviviality started. By nine o'clock Frank, the store man, was telling the Quarter just what he thought of him so Dagnall and I with a little persuasion got his boots off, wrapped a blanket round him and put him to bed with a bottle by his pillow for comfort. He was very soon fast asleep and then we

stood all the empty bottles around him to act as a terrible warning when he woke up the next morning. The following day Sgt Pragnall took what remained up to Brigade. How he has accounted for the missing bottles I don't know.

8.9.18

Wretched weather — rain, thunder and lightning all last night and it has been raining nearly all day. During the night Brigade moved out of the line and now we are near Lijssenthoek, about a mile or so away in a direct line across the fields but two miles by road. Spent much time in letter writing.

12.9.18

Viler than ever today — can't step outside the door without going ankle-deep in watery mud. Have had nearly a week of it now and it's about time we had a change. Last evening it looked as if it were going to be fine so I washed a shirt and two pairs of socks — now they are hanging up in the billet hoping to get dry some day. I think washerwomen ought to go straight to heaven without any examination whatever.

14.9.18

This morning, praise be, there was no rain and soon after breakfast we were on the move again and before noon were located in a barn at the north-west end of Busseboom. I was not satisfied with the place from a Signals' point of view so I strolled round to see what other accommodation was available and soon found that QMS Cass had taken up his abode in a cottage at the south-east end of the village. There was a room in it going spare so I staked my claim and returned to the Transport to fetch down the equipment. Having got comfortably settled in, the next thing to do was to try and get in touch with Brigade. There was a crowd of wires running there and everywhere and they were mostly dud.

Along the road to Ouderdom I found the 123rd Brigade Signal Office. This was a bit of luck, as they had a spare connection on their board and another line direct to my Brigade. So by cutting and joining I got a line back to my billet before nightfall and easily got through to Brigade, much to Sgt Twycross' surprise. It has been a very tiring day, but it would have been worse if it had rained so now (9 p.m.) I am going to 'roost'.

16.9.18
Received a parcel from Elsie containing tobacco (most welcome), papers and a little book of war poems called *Counter-attack* by Siegfried Sassoon. Very good and very outspoken, revealing things as they actually are, not as they are represented to be by the daily press. They will do old Glass-poole's heart good when he reads some of them.

19.9.18

Today we moved half a mile or so to a small cottage on the road to Reninghelst, for what reason is not yet apparent. All the afternoon and evening I was trying to pick up a line that would give me a connection to Brigade but all my endeavours were fruitless and by nightfall I was thoroughly tired out, with the result that when I was standing talking to QMS Cass about 9 p.m. I fell down in a faint, hitting my head a very nice thump on the stone floor. Cass helped me up. Got me to bed and gave me about ¼ of a pint of neat rum and very soon I was fast asleep.

20.9.18

Woke up this morning feeling little the worse for last night's episode. The back of my head is not nearly as tender as I expected it to be; but I have been taking things a little easier today. Took an obscure part in hunting rats with cordite and half a dozen dogs.

23.9.18

After a few days of fine weather, we are again being treated to rain and wind. Some of the fellows got wet through trying to play cricket. Reckon I ought to get my leave in October if the present rate continues, but we can never be sure of anything and when our leave is getting within measurable distance we live in a perpetual state of trembling anxiety which meets with no relief till we are actually on the journey home, armed with all manner of passes and certificates and food coupons. I can feel the wobbly, restless condition coming on me already.

26.9.18
When we came here five days ago we hoped we were going to resume our three weeks' rest which was so rudely broken at the beginning of the month but now the signs of the times are that operations are going to be resumed against the enemy in a few days' time, and consequently we have received orders to move forward tomorrow. I suppose it will mean that leave will be suspended again just as I am beginning to 'sweat' on it earnestly.

27.9.18
Spent most of today in clearing up and packing the wagons. Then, after tea, we commenced our trek towards the line. We went by Abeele station and along the Reninghelst Road, past my old billet at Lappe near which a large Casualty Clearing Station has been built. A nice cheerful sign! Just a little suggestion of what we may be in for. At the bottom of the hill we turned off and went on to Hooggraaf. It was dark by the time we got here. The Transport had to park in a field and of course one of the GS wagons got into a ditch. Before we could get it out, we had to unload it and then as a consequence load it up again. A little matter that caused much cursing in the darkness. Our billet is in a loft, and it is a

tight squeeze. The attack takes place at dawn tomorrow morning and we have to march forward immediately it is launched; so here is one who is going to get some sleep while he may.

28.9.18
At 4 a.m. we were roused and by the light of a few glimmering candles we dressed ourselves and swallowed a hasty breakfast. Then followed the pleasing process of packing the wagons in the dark and getting them out on to the road. As we lined up on the road just before 6 a.m., the roar of artillery started. The depressing spirit of gloom which always sits heavily at these times found expression in Cheesman's words — 'another hopeless dawn, Joe' he said as we looked toward the line where the livid flashes of gunfire were striking up into the sallow dawn. I fell in with the section but Twycross fetched me out to follow the limber. This was the only wagon to accompany us all the way; where the rest went to, I don't know. I didn't greatly relish the job as it made me the very last man in the column — a very undesirable position for when Fritz starts firing at a column on the move it is always the rear part that clocks for the 'dirt'. We passed through Reninghelst, leaving the church on our right, and when we got on to the open road Fritz spotted us and sent over a few HEs. Of course they dropped nearer to me than to anyone else but I was not hit by anything worse than a lump of mud and fortunately Fritz was being kept too busy in other directions to allow

him to pay too much attention to us. After a few miles we put into a camp where we established communication with Division and learned that the attack had been so successful that we were to move forward to Swan Chateau, omitting an intended halt at Ambulance Farm. So on we went past a prisoners of war compound which was getting well filled, until we got there. We remained there for two or three hours, during which time we heard that the attack had met with little resistance and that two or three hundred prisoners were taken in Canada Tunnels.

In getting out from Swan Chateau, one wheel of the limber went into a shell hole and the column had to be halted while a dozen of us pulled it out. I had swung my rifle on the side of the wagon and it came out covered with mud and water so I've got a nice cleaning job to look forward to as soon as we come to rest. For some distance a good plank road helped us along, but once off that the going became a little more strenuous. We were now within the German lines of this morning but there was not the amount of evidence of recent fighting that we had expected. In fact, the number of dead bodies that we passed could be counted on the fingers of one hand. But dusk was shrinking over the land so our powers of vision were limited.

29.9.18
Soon after we were up this morning, a troop of French Cavalry passed by on their way up the

line. A little later we packed up and proceeded to Verbrandenmolen and are now located in a field quite close to the spot we came to last night. Although we were in this neighbourhood in Sept. 1917, I can't say that I recognise the country at all. Hill 60 is just in front of us and Larch Wood slightly to the left with Hedge St Tunnels a little further on. We have found a dugout — it's an English one but Jerry does not seem to have occupied it as it was littered with English papers and periodicals bearing dates early in April, just before Fritz was holding this line. The number of dead is surprisingly small. While prowling round, Cpl Smith found the body of a German Signaller, and searching through his pack discovered a Signal Chart which he gave to me. I shall keep it as a souvenir. It is dreary, desolate, cold and cheerless with plenty of mud and waterlogged shell holes. We are more or less on tenterhooks as we are merely waiting for orders to move forward again. I have no telephone lines, consequently I feel cut off from events and there is nothing to do but play cards, smoke and talk. I'm going to bed, humpy and dumpy and fed up and far from home.

30.9.18
The day was miserably spent in waiting for orders which did not arrive till evening. Then we were ordered to get out on to the road by 9 p.m., ready to move off. It was a wretched business in the dark but by very carefully examining every yard of ground before moving an inch, we

manoeuvred the Signal Limber between the shell holes and got on to the road without mishap. We were the first out, for the other wagons were either less careful or less fortunate and it was 11 p.m. before they were all on the road. Then we started on a most joyless trek. Still, we were thankful that there was no shelling or bombing, neither did it rain. But the mud! For miles we were trudging through thin, watery slush over the tops of our boots and in one place it came up to our knees so that we had to lift up the skirts of our greatcoats to keep them out of it.

1.10.18

As dawn broke, we discovered that our fast-stepping mules had drawn away from the rest of the column which was nowhere in sight. We proceeded slowly until it was quite light without seeing a sign of any other living creature. At last we came to a battery of 18-pdrs drawn up on the roadside. So we halted but could find none of the gunners. So after conferring over a map we turned off along a road that seemed as if it might have been a private road through a gentleman's estate and about 5.30 a.m. we struck Brigade HQ in a farm. There was a sound of cheering when I entered the Signal Office that I gracefully acknowledged and then said, 'Give me something to eat and drink and then let me sleep.' 'No such luck,' said Sgt Twycross, 'we move forward at 6.30 to capture Menin, eleven miles away.' What I said to that I cannot remember and if I could I doubt if I could put it in black and white. I managed, however, to scrounge a cup of tea and a piece of bread off Freddy Moule (the NCOs' cook) and then piled more gear on to the already overloaded limber. It was stacked up nearly five feet high and every jolt or lurch sent my heart up into my mouth. However, there was no help for it, so we set off past a derelict German steam wagon with iron-rimmed wheels evidencing the shortage of rubber. We marched in column of route as we did in Italy, Brigade HQ leading, followed by the Field Ambulance, the Field Co. RE and the three battalions. The morning was fine, the roads were tolerably good and, except for an occasional aeroplane and a little gunfire in the distance, there was no sign of war.

And indeed we weren't expecting any just yet as the Division in front of us reported last night that Wervicq had been cleared of the enemy. So we passed through the ruin of Fenbrielan quite merrily and headed straight for Wervicq. But we had barely got round a bend and within sight of the town when we were met by a hail of machine-gun bullets which brought the column to a dead stop and we made no bones about diving into the ditch that ran beside the road. It was very evident that Fritz was still in Wervicq and that he had been watching us all the way, allowing us to get well within machine-gun range before he gave any notice of his presence. When the burst of firing had died down we continued along the road while the battalions deployed across the fields on our left took some cover from a rise in the ground. Soon I found myself stuck with the wagon at a corner beyond which it was dangerous to go. Sgt Twycross and Cpl Aitken with the Signallers and runners on duty had gone forward; the rest of Brigade HQ and the battalion details had scattered over an adjoining field where some trenches provided a certain amount of shelter. But Lally and I with the limber had to keep to the road and the position was by no means comfortable. The road went uphill from our corner for 200 yards then took a left-hand turn. From that point for about another 100 yards was a death trap. Fritz had some heavy guns trained on it and any troops or wagons that tried to pass along were courting death. I had no desire to run the gauntlet so when Hamilton came across to get some biscuits out of the limber I asked him what I ought to do. 'Stay where you are. There is no need to go any further yet.' We nibbled biscuits and bully and as the day wore on I began to take a great dislike to our position. Several other wagons had lined up behind us and Jerry had a perfectly uninter-rupted view of us. Therefore it seemed improbable that he would let us stand there for ever. His chief observation post is in Wervicq church tower from which point he commands the whole country for a radius, of five to ten miles. During this time there was a steady procession of walking wounded passing us, including Major Puttick of the Hants (wounded in the back) and Blakeway, the KRR runner (wounded in the hand). From him I endeav-oured to get some information as to the whereabouts of Brigade but he was in too much of a hurry to get out of danger. So I learnt nothing.

About 4 p.m. I decided to find out where the rest of the Transport was located, so taking a bicycle I rode back about half a kilometre and found them settling down in a field beside the road. Returning to the limber, I was just giving instructions to Lally to turn round when a 'five-nine' dropped in the gateway on the opposite side of the road about ten yards away. The bits flew over us and round us but nothing more than mud hit us although the tyre of the bicycle I was holding was ripped up. Apparently Fritz thought he had left us alone long enough so we wasted no time in getting out of it. In getting into the Transport Lines, one of the rear wheels of the limber dropped into a ditch and the whole load fell over to one side. Fortunately the mules were able to pull it out and I immediately set to work to unload and repack the stores. I had not finished when six heavy shells burst right amongst us. There was enough explosive mixture to demolish half the Transport but only one man was wounded, and that but slightly, so that he was able to walk away to the dressing station.

Capt. Mowat at once decided that this situation was too exposed so we had the order to move back. We blundered out of the field as quickly as we could and back along a road that was nearly a foot deep in thick, stodgy mud. How I cursed the bicycle I had brought! The wheels were choked up, my strength was almost spent and I could not keep pace with the wagons. But I was able to keep them in view till they turned into a large field. When the limber was safely settled in, I thought it was my duty to report to Brigade so I set off to go up the line. I was starving and utterly tired but I trudged along, passing some 18-pdrs that were putting shrapnel round Wervicq church tower. Up to 6.30 p.m. our artillery had not been allowed to fire at the town because of the civilian inhabitants and even now they were limited to a few rounds of shrapnel at the church tower.

After plodding along for almost a kilometre, I glanced between some huts and who should I see but Hamilton, Davidson and Sgt Lunn. I was now just about exhausted and sank down on to a duckboard, and remained there stretched out at full length while they talked to me. They said there was no need for me to go up the line so I returned to the Transport. We had not had a meal for over twenty-four hours, and had been on the move the whole time so what we said when we heard that there were no rations for us must remain unrecorded. However, there was a sudden rumour that the Officers' rations were in a certain wagon. The driver was enticed away and the rations were ours — bacon and bread and tea. A fire was soon kindled in a hollow and before the loss of rations had been discovered, they were where it was impossible to find them.

2.10.18
Strictly speaking, as there were no rations last night, there ought to have been no breakfast in

350

the morning; but somehow or other tea and sugar were 'procured' and each of us managed to produce a little grub. So at 9 o/c we had a passably good breakfast. The day has been uneventful.

5.10.18
While I was shaving this morning with my mirror on the back of the limber, three of our scouting aeroplanes came up from the rear and met another plane coming from the line. There was the sound of machine-gun firing and we looked up to watch the fight. The single plane tried to get away but one of the Scouts broke from the formation and chased it down to earth. The bullets pinged and zipped all round us and I dived unceremoniously under the wagon. The plane crashed in the next field and then we found it was one of our bombers returning from a night raid with its identification marks camouflaged. The Scouts, not liking the look of it, gave the challenge which the bomber failed to notice. Consequently the Scouts took it to be a Jerry and promptly 'downed' it. There have been several instances lately of Germans flying our machines that they have captured at some point or other. One of the airmen was slightly wounded; the other was unhurt.

6.10.18
Last night no spare accommodation was to be found in the dugouts so Whittingsteel and I had

to unearth a bivouac. We were much too close to the crossroads for comfort. Fritz kept bumping them all night and splinters were dropping all round us but nothing worse than mud or stones hit the 'bivvy'.

During the morning, Brigade moved back, leaving us to follow later. As I had sent Whittingsteel down to B Echelon, Fisher was told off to remain with me. We got on the move after dinner. Through Ypres to Vlamertinghe, where we halted for an hour. We were thirsting for a cup of tea, and prowled about the place in search of a canteen. Found one at last, but it only had beer and biscuits. Dusk was falling when we resumed the march to the farm at Whippenhoek that up to a week or two ago was a Field Ambulance. It was about 8 p.m. when we arrived and we found much excitement over a report that the Germans had asked for an armistice. The optimists crowed loudly and exulted over me for I am credited with being a hopeless pessimist, but it is useless to let desires override one's judgement and I doubt if anything tangible will result from the request (even if it be true). I look on it more as a sign of the beginning of the end, but how long it will be before the end of the end arrives it is impossible to say. I only hope that Germany will realise her doom is sealed and accept the fact very quickly. The march today was twenty miles. Consequently I am not overflowing with energy and shall not be long before I am in bed.

8.10.18

Have just heard that leave has been suspended again — I cannot express myself in words, but I have got the PIP in capital letters and the BLUES also. And this joyful news came along just as I had managed to scrounge a new tunic out of the QMS in anticipation of going on leave, and had paid the Brigadier's batman 3½ francs to make some alterations and sew on new chevrons!

9.10.18

The drivers are getting their leave all right but operators are less fortunate. We poor blighters are practically reduced to 'special cases only'. However, I went and pressed my sad case on Sgt Twycross and as there is only one other man away from the section, he is trying to get my leave sanctioned. I didn't have much trouble in persuading him to do this as he follows me very closely and the sooner I get away, the sooner his own turn will come round.

11.10.18

The truly joyful news has arrived! I am to cross over next Tuesday (15th). Hooray! I am as wibbly-wobbly as a blancmange. Bought a pair of breeches for five francs and made some alterations with my own hand. So I shall look passably respectable which is more than I have done lately for all my clothes were getting ragged and it has been almost impossible to get any new ones from Stores. Brigade go into the line again tomorrow but I am to remain behind as my leave is so near. This is a nice little slice of good fortune.

14.10.18
In accordance with orders, I joined a party of battalion men going on leave just before noon and we set off towards Vlamertinghe. Previously I had confirmed that this was where we were to join the train, but I didn't feel very confident. We had not proceeded more than a kilometre when we met another leave party who also had been sent to Vlam. and they reported that the station was not yet open and they had been instructed to make their way to Poperinghe. So we turned about and trudged along till we were able to 'jump' a lorry that took us to the outskirts of town and we were soon on the station where a number of troops had already congregated. There has been no opportunity this year of getting away a day earlier as I did last year. We entrained at 2 p.m. and reached Calais soon after 8 p.m., the journey being quite uneventful except that we were only six hours in the train instead of eighteen as last year. From Calais station we were marched to a camp near the harbour and put into tents for the night. This is the first time I have been in Calais and the little bit I saw of it did not impress me with its beauty. All the streets we passed through were narrow and almost squalid. Even the best of them had

a very sad and mournful aspect and we were assailed all the way by a host of small children who begged for bully beef or tried to sell us oranges. As soon as we were settled in the camp we were given a meal that we needed rather badly, not having had anything since about 11 a.m. and by half past nine most of us were in our blankets.

15.10.18
Reveille was at the unearthly hour of 5.30 but our breakfast was not till 8 a.m. It turned out that there was another party for Scotland, Ireland and the North of England who were to cross about 9 a.m. Consequently they had to have their breakfast early and with the thoroughness that characterises the army's doings, the whole lot of us were roused at the same time. Of course we had got washed, shaved and cleaned up long before breakfast and there was nothing to do but idle our time away.

Oh, these camps are dismal, desolate holes. Thank goodness we are only birds of passage and don't have to stay in them for many hours at a time. During the afternoon, in calm weather, we crossed over to Dover. There was not much delay here and we were soon speeding on our non-stop journey to London. I reached Ealing at 7.30 p.m. and went straight to Hastings Road where, in the darkness, I knocked at the wrong house. But that little error was soon remedied and I found my Elsie waiting for me.

16.10.18–29.10.18
On leave in England.

30.10.18
I was due to return yesterday but England, home and beauty are very sweet and I took an extra day without asking permission. Elsie came up to Victoria with me and I tried to make things as cheerful as possible by saying that I expect the armistice will be in operation before I get back to my Brigade. Judging from the comments in the press, it certainly seems as if there are definite prospects of an early suspension of hostilities. I don't like to be too optimistic but I doubt if the fighting will last for more than another month or six weeks at the latest. Yet this bright possibility does not seem to meet with much favour in the eyes of the stay-at-home community. Work people have been getting big wages on war work, employers have been piling up huge profits, and industrial adventurers have waxed fat out of the agony and suffering of the five million poor devils who have made the human wall that for over four years has protected the profiteer, the adventurer and the shirker from the violence and ravages of the Hun. And now they realise that this profitable period is soon to close and they begin to squeal. What will they do if there is no war? And what will happen to them when the armies return home? They shiver in their shoes. They don't want us to come back. The attitude of England towards the British Tommy today is 'Hurry up and get killed before the war is over'.

We did not stay long at Dover. The crossing was perfect — the sea as calm as a lake — the sun shining brightly. I remained on deck to enjoy the sea air. At Calais we were soon plunged into the cheerfulness of the reception camp, but we are off tomorrow morning. Thank goodness we don't have to stay long in these places.

31.10.18
Entrained during the morning and were taken up through St Omer, Hazebrouk (badly knocked about), Poperinghe and Ypres. Jolly glad that the railway has been reconstructed right over Passchendaele Ridge. We had to travel slowly as it is none too safe. Near Passchendaele I was looking out of the truck and saw George Thompson working with a Labour Battalion. We exchanged greetings — that was all we had time to do. And so on to Roulers about dusk, eventually arriving at Ledeghem at 9 p.m. In Ypres I noticed that a few civilians have already drifted back. They are living in covered-in wagons.

At Ledeghem we were marched to the far end of the town and put into what had been one of Fritz's Civilian Internment Camps. Our reception was not the sort associated with open arms and fatted calves. We were just dumped into a large shed that was fitted with wire-netting beds and told that reveille would be at 6 a.m. No food, no blankets! We approached all the Camp NCOs we could find but were met with blank refusals to issue any blankets. We were not feeling any too happy and satisfied and soon the murmured protests began to grow until there was a very nice-sized uproar and some Haw-Haw Officer came in and tried to ride the high horse, demanding our pay books and threatening us with punishment. But he didn't get a single pay book and he had sense enough to realise the rising temper of the troops and accordingly gave orders for us to be supplied with blankets. If he had not done this I'm afraid there would have been something in the nature of a mutiny.

1.11.18

About 8.30 a.m. we turned our backs on Ledeghem and marched to Courtrai, the largest town I have passed through in Belgium. This place was captured by 122nd Brigade 41st Division only a few days ago. There is much evidence of Fritz's retirement. He has blown up all the bridges and railway station and has done a lot of damage to the permanent way. Large gangs of men were busy at work on Courtrai station. One thing that struck us as remarkable is the large number of Allied flags that are flying in every town, village and hamlet through which we pass. (It turned out that this was an instance of Fritz's business acumen. When retirement was inevitable he sent his bagman with loads of Allied flags and sold them to the natives!) At Courtrai our party was split up, men of different divisions going their several ways.

A limber went by going to 122nd Brigade so

we dumped our packs on it. I also scrounged a tin hat from the roadside as I had purposely left mine at home, knowing full well that I should be able to pick one up somewhere or other before I got into the line. Jimmy Bissett arrived on the scene and told me that Brigade is somewhere near Kerkove but he could give me no definite information except that Fritz is holding us up on the Scheldt. We got on the move again and soon passed through one or two villages where chalk marks on doors gave evidence of recent occupation by some of our battalions. Beyond this we were not fortunate for dusk found us stranded near a few cottages. We were very fatigued and after a consultation with our officer it was decided to find shelter for the night and continue our journey in the morning. The march today covered sixteen miles.

2.11.18
We were glad of the abundance of straw last night for we had no blankets. So we just buried ourselves in the straw and slept well except for an occasional disturbance by one of Fritz's bombing aeroplanes that were busy in the neighbourhood.

Some rations had been procured from somewhere so we had breakfast and then set off again on our search for the 122nd Brigade. We had only gone a mile or two when we found them established in a chateau. Had a look at Company Orders and observed that a driver at Division got fourteen days' FP No. 1 for overstaying his leave twenty-four hours. Just then Sgt Twycross came along and asked for my pass. I felt in all my pockets and couldn't find it. He said the authorities are being very severe on men who have overstayed their leave and he asked me what day I left London. I told him a lie without the least sign of guilt and he made the necessary report to Division. Then I went out into a quiet corner and burnt that pass with the incriminating date stamped on it at Victoria and the burnt ashes I crumpled in my hands and scattered to the winds.

Davidson is on leave. His father died a week or so ago so he got his leave earlier than would otherwise have been the case. Glasspoole is also on leave. He has 'clicked' for six weeks owing to his Yeomanry Service. Aitken has gone to England to take a commission in the RAF and during my absence I have been lifted into his place with the rank of L/Cpl. The appointment dates from 18 October. Had no idea that anything of the sort was in the air. Jack Carter has also been promoted to Lineman L/Cpl.

The lid has come off the tin of cold cream in my pocket and the stuff has got mixed up with tobacco dust.

3.11.18
Our men captured a most extraordinary bicycle from the enemy; we have got it standing just outside the door of the chateau. It is more evidence of the serious shortage of rubber in Germany, for instead of the ordinary tyres the

rim of each wheel is surmounted with a number of helical springs bound together by an exterior band of iron. (Later we saw many of these. The Belgians appropriated them, and they made a truly awful clatter on the pavé).

5.11.18
Our progress was not very rapid as a great number of troops were on the road. At one point somebody's transport had been badly knocked about as several dead horses were lying by the roadside. The first one we saw had lost the whole of one hind leg and we rather marvelled at such extraordinary mutilation. But we passed three or four others in exactly the same condition and we learned that the natives had cut off the hindquarters and carted them away for food. The afternoon was well advanced before we reached Harlebeke. Our billet is in a quite respectable house but some distance from the Signal Office.

6.11.18
Weather very cheerless — raining fast all day and we are glad that we did the march yesterday. Now that we have got away from the stretch of country desolated by four years of continual trench warfare, we look like getting much better billets although there is more moving about to do. In fact this open warfare is infinitely preferable to the nerve-shattering, muddy, filthy and poisonous warfare of the trenches. There is

nothing like the same amount of shellfire to contend with and now that we know that we have got Fritz beaten we suffer no apprehensions, when turning in at night, that we shall find him a little too near to us for comfort in the morning.

7.11.18

Some of the runners discovered great piles of books in the attic of our billet. Immediately I heard of it I hastened to the scene and found a wonderful collection of books, mostly theological, in English, French, German, Flemish and Latin. It was delicious to turn over volume after volume, reading a bit here and a bit there. Two huge, rather ancient Psalters attracted my attention but they were too big and heavy to appropriate. Selected a French book on physiology and Hamilton and I have spent some time in translating it. The Huns have definitely asked for an armistice and we have had orders to look out for their emissaries coming over with a white flag but it is not anticipated that they will cross over on our front. Operations, however, are not to be suspended and there is to be no relaxation in our attacks. This is hard luck as we are still held up on the Scheldt and now we (the 122nd Brigade) have got to force the passage. I must admit that I don't view the prospect with the least bit of enthusiasm as I shall have to take the Forward Party over.

It's bad enough attacking on dry land or in knee-deep mud, but when you have got to get across a wide swiftly flowing river on a pontoon bridge hastily thrown across, with Fritz directing all his attention on that point, you can't feel that your chances of coming through are particularly rosy.

This is a larger town than we usually get billeted in and it seems to be quite an ecclesiastical centre. There are crowds of priests and church officials and one old boy (possibly a bishop as he wears a mitre) who shuffles about town preceded by a small boy carrying a lantern and ringing a bell. On his approach, men and women go down on their knees in the muddy gutter and he mutters blessings over them. It certainly looks grotesque and it struck Bill Rogers as distinctly funny. He thought at first that it had something to do with Guy Fawkes Day! The funeral of a Belgian soldier was an opportunity for the ecclesiastics to make a brave show, four or five priests intoning Latin chants in raucous tones, yet doing it heartily withal. A detachment of British troops acted as a firing party.

9.11.18
Early today it was evident that there was something 'in the wind' and during the morning we received the order to stand by. Later we were ordered to pack up and be ready to move, and accordingly in the early afternoon we marched off a distance of eight miles. The latter part of the journey was rather rough especially where we had to pass under the railway. Fritz had blown

the bridge up and we had to clamber over heaps of masonry. The greatest difficulty was in getting the wagons over but it was all accomplished without mishap. It was getting dusk when we reached the farm and we quickly perceived that the old farmer and his family did not welcome our arrival. This attitude was explained later when we learnt that last night a unit of the 9th Division was billeted here and the fellows fairly looted the place, milking the cows on to the ground, breaking all the eggs and ransacking the house. It is always a curse to follow one of these Hooligan Divisions.

10.11.18
Up very early, according to plan, and soon the news came through that Fritz had retired from the Scheldt during the night. I, for one, heaved many sighs of relief. It was daylight when we got on the move again and continued our march to the Scheldt where we found that the Engineers had already thrown across a footbridge and had repaired the demolished road bridge sufficiently to carry light transport. The approach to the river was over marshy land and we were unfortunate to get held up for a few minutes. This was sufficient to allow the wagons to begin sinking into the mud and it required the help of all available men to pull them out. The river runs swift and cold and deep and we shuddered as we passed over it thinking of what might have been our fate. Once across, however, we struck a good road and continued merrily until we reached

Sulsique. It is remarkable that we have not seen a single scrap of war material except huge shells used for mining the crossroads. Fritz seems to have cleared the country of everything before he retired. We were directed to take a short cut across some fields while the Transport went round by the road. We had to jump a stream and struggle up a steep hill and so into a lane that was a foot deep in thick, stodgy mud. It was terribly hard work at the end of a tiring day and it was impossible to push the bicycles. It needed three men to pull each one. Eventually we reached a good road and lined up, a very worn and weary looking crowd. A few cheery words from Mr Bell, telling us that we were nearing the end of our day's march, put a little life in us and we plodded on to Nukerke in the moonlight, arriving there about 7 p.m., the Transport putting in an appearance about an hour later. Our billet is in an estaminet kept by two elderly ladies who seem very nervous and fearful. After getting our packs from the wagon we wasted very little time in getting into our blankets, sleeping on the straw on which Germans slept last night.

11.11.18 Armistice Day

I was sorry for the men on duty last night, especially the runners, for they were kept on the go all night long and Bill Rogers, who normally should have turned in soon after 10 p.m., had to remain on duty throughout the night. Consequently at 8 a.m. I went on duty and relieved him. We were anxiously awaiting orders when about 8.30 [the 122nd Infantry Brigade War Diary states that the signal was received at 09.08] the 'Sounder' started to tap. Campbell was the Divisional Operator on duty and as the instrument ticked I read off 'Hostilities will cease . . . ' That was enough. I had to suppress the jubilation in the Office in order to give Campbell a chance to get his message off. Before he had finished, the Office was crowded with enquirers. Mr Bell came in and took the telegram while I appropriated a copy (I kept this until some months after I got home and then it mysteriously disappeared and although I have turned the whole house inside out three or four times there is no trace of it anywhere). The excitement among the troops was not great; indeed, except for a little spasmodic jubilation here and there, no difference in the ordinary behaviour of the men is to be observed. It is just taken as a matter of course. The two old ladies of the estaminet hardly know where they are. For the past week they have been living more or less in a state of terror, not understanding what was happening and spending sleepless nights because of the noise of the guns. When we told them the good news they broke down and cried. We gave them jam and cheese, luxuries that they had not enjoyed for years and in return they gave us some apples which they had kept hidden from Fritz.

The language of the neighbourhood is Flemish but one of the old dames speaks French, so we are able to make each other understood. Their chief concern last night when we arrived was